TRANSFORMATIVE

INITIATION

FOR

WITCHES

About the Author

Frater Barrabbas Tiresius is a practicing ritual magician who has studied magic and the occult for over forty years. He believes that ritual magic is a discipline whose mystery is unlocked by continual practice and by occult experiences and revelations. Frater Barrabbas believes that traditional approaches should be balanced with creativity and experimentation, and that no occult or magical tradition is exempt from changes and revisions.

Over the years, he found that his practical magical discipline was the real source for all his creative efforts. That creative process helped him build and craft a unique and different kind of magical system, one that is quite unlike any other yet based on common Wiccan practices. So, despite its uniqueness this magical system is capable of being easily adapted and used by others.

Frater Barrabbas is also the founder of a magical order called the Order of the Gnostic Star and he is an elder and lineage holder in the Alexandrian tradition of Witchcraft.

TRANSFORMATIVE INITIATION FOR WITCHES

THE ART OF MASTERING INNER CHANGE

FRATER BARRABBAS

Chicago, Illinois

Paperback ISBN: 978-1-959883-30-2
Library of Congress Control Number on file.

Cover design by Wycke Malliway.
Edited by Becca Fleming.
Typesetting by Gianna Rini.

Published by:
Crossed Crow Books, LLC
6934 N Glenwood Ave, Suite C
Chicago, IL 60626
www.crossedcrowbooks.com

Printed in the United States of America.

Other Books by Frater Barrabbas

Mastering the Art of Witchcraft, Crossed Crow Books
Sacramental Theurgy for Witches, Crossed Crow Books
Talismanic Magic for Witches, Llewellyn
Elemental Powers for Witches, Llewellyn
Spirit Conjuring for Witches, Llewellyn
Magical Qabalah for Beginners, Llewellyn

Forthcoming Titles

Mastering the Art of Ritual Magick, Crossed Crow Books
The Disciple's Guide to Ritual Magick, Crossed Crow Books
Liber Nephilim, Crossed Crow Books

DEDICATION

This book is dedicated to the memory of Donna Schulze (Gardnerian Initiatrix and magical pioneer), Maxine Sanders, and James Baker, to my wife Joni, who taught me how to write books, and to Lynxa, my feline muse.

ACKNOWLEDGMENTS

Many thanks to Keith Ward for his artistic assistance and visions, to Aidan Kelly for his informative book about the various renditions of the Gardnerian Book of Shadows, and to Joseph Campbell for writing his book, Hero with a Thousand Faces, which set me on my current path so many years ago.

CONTENTS

A Note from the Author. . . . . *xiii*

Introduction: What Is Initiation—A Definition 1

PART ONE: TRADITIONAL INITIATION

Chapter One: British Traditional Witchcraft—
Three Initiation Ordeals 13
    Initiation as Cultic Entry and Privilege 15
    Initiation Critique and the Masonic Connection 19
    Missing Third Ordeal. 26

Chapter Two: The Third Ordeal Initiation
for Modern Witchcraft 31

Chapter Three: Non-Traditional Initiations—
Beyond Third Degree. 41
    The Fourth Degree Initiation and Ritual Pattern 44
    The Fifth Degree Initiation and Ritual Pattern 51
    Guardian and Priest/ess of the Mysteries 59
    Monarch of the Mysteries 62
    Hierophant Master of the Mysteries 66

Chapter Four: Essential Attributes of Initiation 69
    Declaration and Building an Identity. 74
    Dedication to the Deities of Witchcraft. 76
    Building a Practice and Self-Initiation. 80
    Community Work and Mentorship 83

Chapter Five: Self-Initiation and Magical Initiation
of the Four Elements Rite 89
  Passage Through the Four Elements. 90
  Goddesses and Gods of the Four Seasons. 93
  Ritual of the Self-Initiation of the Four Elements. 95

PART TWO: TRANSFORMATIONAL INITIATION

Chapter One: What is Transformative
Initiation—A Definition 105
  Madness and Apotheosis 109
  Depression and the Dark Night of the Soul 112
  Pathway of Spiritual Ascension and
    the Way of Witchcraft. 118

Chapter Two: Hero's Journey and the Cosmogonic Cycle 121
  Hero's Journey and the Fool's Journey 123
  Twenty-Two Stages of the Hero's Journey
    and the Tarot Trumps 126
  Part I—The Separation or Departure 129
  Part II—The Trials and Victories of Initiation 132
  Part III—The Cosmogonic Cycle;
    the Vision that is the Hero's Boon. 138
  Part IV—The Return and Reintegration with Society. 141
  Tarot Trumps and the Cycle of Initiation 145

Chapter Three: Heroine's Journey and the
Feminine Initiation Cycle 149
  Body of Woman as Avatar—the Visionary Mystery 154
  Heroine Cycle Stage One—
    Marriage to Death and the Serpent's Temptation 155
  Heroine Cycle Stage Two—
    Trials of Love and Restoration. 157
  Heroine Cycle Stage Three—
    Ascent: Daughter as Mother 158

Chapter Four: Invocation of Personal Transformation
Using the Tarot Trumps 161
   Knowing the Stage of Your Initiatory Process 164
   Ritual Tarot Pathworking. 166
   Double Tetrahedral Gateway Vortex Ritual 168

Conclusion: Initiation and Transformation
in Modern Witchcraft 173

Bibliography. *179*
Index *181*

A Note from the Author

W hen I wrote the previous four books in the *For Witches* series, I had some material left over that I thought was very important. These chapters just didn't fit into any of the previous books, so I thought that I would just shelve them and end my series with the book *Sacramental Theurgy for Witches*. I believed that these four books covered the topics that I wanted to explore and that the topics of initiation, particularly transformational initiation and how it matched up with the literary Hero's Journey would be used in some other series, or perhaps not at all. After all, I did cover these concepts in a previous work (*Mastering the Art of Ritual Magick*), but I did not cover them from the perspective of modern Witchcraft or Paganism, nor did I cover them in the detail that I had desired. I also wrote those sections in that book from the perspective of a ritual magician of any faith.

Still, I thought that someone else would probably write up books highlighting these topics since there are so many books and materials about traditional and non-traditional Witchcraft in print or available online. I was at peace with what I had produced so far, but I now realize that my muse, whose unknown presence often haunts my dreams and imaginings, was not yet finished with this series.

What happened to me is that when I was relaxing in a darkened room, lying on a massage table while undergoing the quiet period following an acupuncture treatment that my mind was filled with the inspired visions of this fifth book, *Transformational Initiation for Witches*. I not only produced the title for the book but also its contents. When I got home, I wrote down notes about what I had experienced, and the table of contents seemed to manifest while I was writing my impressions. I had gotten an inspiration in that moment of total relaxation despite having needles sticking in my flesh, and I sought to fully realize it.

Many years ago, when I was initiated into Witchcraft, I had a profound and moving experience. That moment changed my life forever. Even though I had been engaging in Witchcraft magic for a few years before that time, getting my initiation seemed to pull everything together for me in a way that I had never experienced before. Later, attending other people's initiations in the coven seemed less dramatic and profound to me, but still were charged with transformative powers. However, when I sat down to transcribe my Book of Shadows from the coven copy, I discovered that not only had my initiation differed somewhat from what was written in the book, but the text itself was so rudimentary and functionally basic that I was surprised that it had any effect on me at all. It was a puzzle to me at the time and one that I was not able to understand until some years later.

I had read the book by Joseph Campbell, *The Hero with a Thousand Faces* prior to getting initiated, but it wasn't until a bit later when I discovered that the literary cycle of the hero had overall twenty-two stages that I was able to compare it to the same number of Tarot trump cards. I found that they matched after a fashion. That discovery helped me to realize that the Hero's Journey, as depicted in the Tarot, was the same as what I imagined was the cycle of initiation. Further research and working with the cards in that manner allowed me a degree of confidence that what I had discovered was a breakthrough and an especially useful method for self-analysis and triggering internal psychic transformations.

Armed with that knowledge, I examined the scripted initiation rituals of my tradition and found similar symbols and metaphors operating in them. I also traced the history of these initiation rites that Gerald B. Gardner had fashioned to their source, which were two of the three initiations of Blue Lodge Masonry. I had read a couple of other articles that pointed to these rituals as the source for Witchcraft initiations, so I did the research and found it to be true. That made me realize that the legitimacy of Witchcraft initiations was based on the authenticity of the Masonic initiations, so I could, if needed, modify, enhance, and build up new initiation lore. I was behaving in an unorthodox manner, but I felt that Witches were supposed to be opposed to orthodoxy.

Transformative Initiation for Witches relies to some extent on the previous book, *Sacramental Theurgy for Witches* since the art of consecration, godhead assumption, and the Mysteries of the moon and sun, play a significant part in the initiation cycle of everyone who is on the initiatory path of Witchcraft and Paganism. These practices and arts become even more important when the practitioner is a solitary and self-initiated Witch or Pagan. I would recommend that the reader of this book also read and study the work *Sacramental Theurgy for Witches* since it will explain what is referenced and assumed in this work.

This book contains the legacy of those years of research and development and offers the reader a two-part analysis and presentation of the scripted rituals of initiation and the stages of the process of psychic transformation. I believe that this work will not only find a home for the writings that did not make it into my previous four works, but it will present the ideas and practices that I have been using for decades to expand Witchcraft initiations. These techniques allowed me to control the process of psychic transformation, making them a powerful tool to be used on myself and on others who might be undergoing a difficult transition.

Frater Barrabbas

WHAT IS INITIATION— A DEFINITION

"The master initiate of any Craft appears
magical to the uninitiated."

BRYANT MCGILL

In modern Witchcraft, initiation means many things to many people. Those who belong to the British Traditional Witchcraft (BTW) lineage subscribe to three degrees and use them to denote different levels of ability, accomplishment, and seniority. A first-degree Witch is a kind of apprentice and a second- or third-degree Witch is an experienced practitioner and coven group or tradition leader. For Gardnerians, a third-degree High Priestess is considered a lineage holder, and it is through her that everyone in the coven has their pedigree and relative legitimacy. It is neither the coven nor the High Priest who has any precedence in these considerations; to the Gardnerian, one's spiritual and magical inheritance rests in the hands of the High Priestess who sets their magic circle for the initiation rite.

The online Merriam-Webster dictionary defines initiation in the following manner.

> *"[T]he rites, ceremonies, ordeals, or instructions with which one is made a member of a sect or society or is invested with a particular function or status."[1]*

---

1   Editorial Staff, "Initiation," Merriam Online Dictionary, accessed February 12, 2023. https://www.merriam-webster.com/dictionary/initiation

According to this definition, a Witchcraft initiation is a ritual conducted by officiating members of a group (coven) to make an outsider a member and to invest that individual with the privileges and status associated with that sect or society. What this means is that the members have the authority to change the status of an outsider to that of a member of the group. The process of being made a member may entail ordeals, instructions, or teachings, performed in a solemn and ceremonial manner. The ordeals may consist of a spiritual dedication, swearing oaths of fidelity and secrecy, and enduring challenging physical disabilities and hardships, such as being naked, bound, and blindfolded, and being scourged, set upon with a sword or dagger, as well as being anointed, embraced, empowered, uplifted, and welcomed into the group. A Witchcraft initiation is in many ways like an initiation into a secret society, which is what the original traditional initiation rites were modeled after.

While such an initiation ordeal is quite dramatic and seemingly life-changing, it does not bestow upon the initiated any powers or prerogatives other than what is included in the membership and knowledge of the group. A traditional initiation rite then, by itself, does not bestow spiritual wisdom or any kind of magical or spiritual realization. The ritual does nothing to change the individual who undergoes it other than make them a member of the social group and tradition and give them a certain recognition or status within that group. A person could, therefore, attain a very high status in their group or community, yet lack any kind of specialized spiritual skills or magical ability.

What I am not saying is that an initiation rite won't have any effect on the one who undergoes it. Many individuals experience profound insights, visions, and sensations, and can even discuss how the event changed their lives. These kinds of occurrences do happen, and they happen more often than producing no effect. What I am attempting to state is that the initiation rite by itself does not guarantee that such a powerful occurrence will, in fact, occur. There is obviously something that is happening to a Candidate when they are initiated that has more to do with their own stage of growth and knowledge and the context and sensory impressions of the event. Something internal is happening while the initiation rite is performed, but that phenomenon is individual, personal, and intimate.

I have known individuals who underwent traditional initiations and who felt no differently afterward as if the initiation had no lasting or long-term effect or impact on them. Still others, including myself, were profoundly impacted by what they experienced in their initiation rite. Traditional initiations have a role to play, depending on the tradition that one follows, but they cannot confer any kind of internal change since they are scripted and not varied for the individual. Initiations can trigger something else to happen, but that is dependent on the individual and their internal psychic process.

As I said in my many books and articles, because Witchcraft is a magical religion, having expertise in magical workings as well as wisdom and insight are part of the overall process of development. An initiation cannot confer that kind of expertise or spiritual accomplishment. Only hard work, constant effort, and years of practice will assist one in achieving that kind of capability. Yet there is another process involved in the Mystery of initiation and how it affects individuals.

There are also assumptions associated with being an Initiate versus not being initiated. In the early years of modern Witchcraft, those who were not initiated were outsiders. They couldn't claim any of the powers or knowledge of the Witchcraft tradition. There was a certain level of smug superiority between someone who had been initiated as opposed to the masses who weren't so blessed. There were authentic Witches and there were pretenders or fraudulent claimants. A lot of acrimony was spent on the declaration of authenticity or the debunking of some teacher's legitimacy. I found this kind of activity to be irrelevant since it seemed to me that legitimacy was a subjective quality based wholly on the spiritual and magical abilities that someone who called themselves a Witch could demonstrate. Some folks still think that pedigree and legitimacy are important, while others have moved on to what they think is more important.

Over the years, I have found that some folks who have never been initiated have more knowledge, experience, and personal depth than someone who is named a Witch Queen and has several covens who owe fealty to her. Some people are very much into the social structure of covens and communities, others are into the religious aspects of Witchcraft, and still others are into the practice of magic. Some approach Witchcraft with both a religious and a practical magical perspective. I find myself in that category. Yet, for those who practice magic and who seek alignment and union with the Deities, the work will, over time and even unwittingly, foster dramatic and unscripted changes in them.

Where initiation is limited to a social organization and its periodic practices, any kind of dramatic and constructive change in a member will be unplanned and fortuitous. When it includes the practice of magic and sacramental theurgy, then it will cause profound internal changes either by planned deliberation or theistic intervention. There would appear to be, then, two kinds of initiations that are possible for the Witch who practices magic and religious rites conjoined. There are the obvious initiations of the tradition and another lesser-known or discussed initiation associated with a process of psychological transformation. It is my premise that when one experiences a profound transformation during a traditional initiation rite, then both types of phenomena, cultic ordeal, and internal change are happening at the same time.

Where traditional initiations have written rituals and a body of lore to support them, transformative initiations have no such body of lore. They are mostly unwritten and truly mysterious. To understand the unwritten transformative initiation, we must scrutinize the documented initiation rituals and add some very important features to our knowledge. I have found that transformative initiation is cyclic and that it follows the mythic cycle of the hero in the literary tradition.

This transformative cycle is obliquely found in the symbols and the narrative of known initiation rites, although it is not always recognizable as such. It is also found in the mythic cosmogonic cycles of the early religions of the world. It is an ancient body of lore that represents the cycle of psychic rebirth from psychological disintegration, death, and collapse. It is madness and it is redemption, the occurrence of enlightenment and spiritual ascension. This process is not the sole practice of the mystic or the religious ascetic, it is also shared with the practitioner of religious magic who is continually exposed to the transformative powers of the Deity.

Those Witches who practice magic and sacramental theurgy are individuals who often experience the endless cycles of transformative initiation throughout their lives. Once they begin this practice, the outcome of internal psychic challenges, tragedies, victories, and endless change is inescapable. While this might be the lot of practically all human beings, engaging in the regimen of religious magic makes the experiences more dramatic and intensive. To endure this endless cycle of transformations, the Witch must be steadfast in their religious devotions, spiritual alignments, magical workings, and sacramental offerings. This is because it is the mystery and magic of the Deities and the Witch's faith that keeps them buoyant while undergoing these continual transformative perturbations.

Scripted initiation and transformative initiation are two sides to the same psychological and spiritual coin. The first represents a social transition and recognition, and the second represents the process of growth and ultimate transcendence. Behind both processes are the symbols of transformation, as C. G. Jung called them, that can trigger internal processes that are continually occurring, whether as static potentials or activated psychic events. We should examine these symbols of transformation as they appear in the traditional initiation rites of Witchcraft, as established by Gardner, as well as realize them in the stages of the Hero's Journey. To master these symbols of transformation that so powerfully affect the inner self or soul is to master one's own transformational process or to trigger and guide it for another person.

Initiation also serves two kinds of coven organizations. There is the teaching coven that seeks to initiate and train new Witches to master the arts of the Craft, and once they achieve their three degrees, they will leave the coven to form their own coven, thereby making the High Priestess a potential lineage holder over multiple covens. The other coven type is the senior group, where the members progress through all three degrees so that all might explore the Mysteries and magic of the Craft fully as equals.

A teaching coven is always open to new members and relies on traditional scripted initiation rites, and a senior coven is closed after the basic number of members has been admitted and relies on developed and discovered lore to continue growth, often including non-scripted transformative initiations. Some covens start as teaching covens and then later become closed to new members once they have achieved a majority of third-degree members. Yet, only a senior-styled coven can seek to explore the powers and Mysteries of transformative initiation or develop initiations and lore beyond the third degree.

The purpose of this book, then, is to explore both the scripted traditional initiation rituals and their ancillary practices and rites and to explore the unscripted transformation process that can be triggered or guided magically, but never forced or encapsulated in written rituals. We will analyze and discover the symbols of transformation that seem to embody both the scripted initiation rite and imbed the transformational initiation process to uncover and reveal the actual Mystery of initiation.

Yet what is behind those powerful archetypes is the activated experience of the Deities and their profound impact on human consciousness. I would surmise that the process of initiation is the Mystery of the revelation of the Deity within the individual, as well as the effect that realization has on the person and their life process. Those who seem to be most deeply impacted by an initiation are those who have a strong alignment with the Deities, and those who merely walk through an initiation without experiencing any profound internal changes are those who have a limited, weak, or blocked connection with the Goddesses and Gods of the Witchcraft cult. I believe that the process of learning and experiencing the Deity within oneself is an important key to how much of an impact an initiation will have on a person undergoing it.

One of the most important things for me to discuss here is that internal change is difficult and painful. Many people ignore the signs that a necessary change within their being is at the threshold of their lives. Change often signifies that one's opinions, beliefs, and lifestyle are somehow wrong or headed in the wrong direction. To admit that lifestyle changes or a change in one's attitudes or opinions are necessary is likely the most difficult thing that a person could be forced to do. For instance, someone could have a sweet tooth and discover later that they are diabetic, or a heavy smoker discovering that they are beginning to show signs of emphysema; they will have to change their habits to continue to live. These are the obvious changes that must be seriously considered, but then there are the more subtle changes.

Such a subtle change requirement would be when a person unwittingly exhibits sexist or racist behavior in the workplace or polite society. Behavior like that might require a change for the person exhibiting it so they would be able to have diverse relationships or achieve the desired results in their career. Some people might realize their behavior is a problem and others might steadfastly refuse to change and blame society for making them feel bad about themselves.

If it is difficult for many people to be able to change their habits due to health reasons or social conflicts, then think how difficult it would be for someone to realize that they need to change for the sake of their mental health. Human nature, as such, tends to resist change. People resist change until either a catastrophic event occurs or tragedy envelopes them, forcing them to change. Thus, change is considered something bad or something to completely avoid if possible.

The willingness to undergo an initiation or experience a powerful internal transformation represents that a person is open and willing to allow themselves to be vulnerable, to let go of their past, and to make a course correction in their lives. They allow their old selves to be sacrificed to realize a new aspect of themselves—a new personality and a changed life path. Obviously, seeking such an outcome requires courage and faith in oneself. The important consideration is that we must always be open to change, grow, and spiritually evolve. We cannot stubbornly hang on to our beliefs, habits, and opinions if we are seeking to engage and experience the beingness of the Deities and the domain of the spirit world.

If we are resistant to change, then when change occurs, it is more intense, painful, and difficult. The underlying lesson here is that change in the material world is a fact of life, and we cannot resist it unless we imperil ourselves. This is also true deep within our psyches; change is happening whether we embrace or reject it. If change is a fact of life, then the only problem we must resolve is understanding that we are not changeless nor immortal. Yet it is more difficult for people to accept this truth than it is to continue living as if we were immune to change and invulnerable to death. What it requires is a kind of detachment or an acceptance of the impermanence of all things, including our conscious selves.

Therefore, scripted initiation, transformative initiation, and an openness and willingness to change are the hallmarks of this hallowed process. Still, not everything occurs smoothly and without trauma or pain in an initiation, especially when one is gripped in an unscripted and unexpected transformation. There is often some degree of resistance and disbelief that must be overcome, and the disintegration of the old self is not a pleasant experience. The downward spiral of the self as it implodes is painful since it is a psychic death and there is no guarantee that a person will overcome this process and ascend into a newly reborn self. The initial pathway of transformation is the same for someone who is evolving or devolving; it is that slight difference that makes for a spiritual rebirth or the descent into madness. Since there is never a guarantee that the transformative cycle will be resolved with a spiritual rebirth, there is an inherent accompanied fear and even terror associated with the process of psychic death.

We will seek to understand this process of internal psychic change, and through that understanding, we might also realize the fragility and vulnerability of the human psyche. Knowing how to use the symbols of transformation in a constructive and insightful way will help us to understand this mysterious process that can aid or destroy us. A strong spiritual alignment with the Deities can certainly help us to experience a constructive transformation, yet so can a strong will and self-determination. All three of these characteristics joined together can help the one undergoing a transformation to achieve a positive outcome. It will change the Initiate from being a victim to becoming a savior to themself. All these preparations, rites, disciplines, and teachings about scripted initiations and transformative initiations will assist the spiritual seeker in mastering their own spiritual path. This, then, is the objective of this work—to master the powers and wisdom of transformative initiation so that Witches might guide and direct themselves as well as others.

This book has two parts, representing the differences between scripted initiation rites and the process of transformative initiation. They are tied to each other through the kinds of symbols and metaphors employed, but they represent two distinct processes in the spiritual awakening and experiential-based growth of the Witch. We will explore the traditional initiation rituals and practices, as well as the non-traditional or extra-traditional ones. We will question the importance of scripted initiations, present the possibilities and rituals for self-initiation, and we will also examine the hypothetical initiations for higher degrees. More importantly, we will analyze the symbols and metaphors contained in traditional initiations to understand the symbols of transformation employed in them. The first part examines what is truly known about traditional and non-traditional scripted initiations, then the second part examines the transformational initiation.

The second part of this book will introduce the cycle of the Hero's Journey, fully examine that pattern, and discuss how it relates to the stages of psychic transformation. Additionally, I will show how this pattern of twenty-two stages (the Hero's Cycle in seventeen stages and the cosmogonic cycle in five stages) aligns with the twenty-two trumps of the standard Tarot deck. We are fortunate that the Tarot trumps fit into this pattern and can give the greater and lesser cycles contained therein a rich symbolic content of images and metaphors that they might otherwise not possess. It is my belief that the symbols of transformation that activate transformative initiation are depicted in the symbology of the Tarot trumps. They can also be used as magical tools to both query one's internal process and trigger transformative changes that are needed to continue to grow and awaken. The second part of this book goes hand and glove with the first part because initiation should be a continual process that produces incremental constructive changes that empower and strengthen the initiate.

We will consider all these topics in the following chapters of this book. I believe that writing such a book, even though it discusses topics that are very close to what would be considered oath-bound material, is essential because transformational initiation—and its counterpart, scripted initiation rituals—are the least understood practices in the various traditions of Witchcraft and Paganism. There are critical underlying elements to be discovered and documented while examining both processes, and as I have said, when one masters these processes, then one has acquired the key to wisdom, psychic endurance, and life-based experiential enlightenment.

To ask a question about something that is either obscure or taken for granted, such as psychic transformation and initiation, is to begin the insightful process of learning, and ultimately, to answer that question. I believe that modern Witches and Pagans should understand and realize the importance of scripted initiations, but also how they function and how they can impact the Candidate. Possessing this knowledge would allow someone to refine or even write their own initiations. I know that such a statement is controversial, and you may ask yourself, who would deem themselves to have the proper authority to make changes to what has been traditionally passed down from their teachers? The answer is that there is no final authority in our traditions unless we believe there is one. At the very least, we can understand how these scripted initiations work.

We hold in our hands a tradition passed down to us that was rudimentary and incomplete. This has certainly been accepted as true for the eight sabbat rites, but it is also true for the initiation rites. Adding and refining these rituals might be considered unorthodox, but I find the concept of an orthodox Witchcraft to be an oxymoron. The words *orthodox* and *Witchcraft* should never be used in the same sentence because they are mutually opposed, similar to Orthodox Christianity being opposed by the rebellion or counter-revolution of Witchcraft and Paganism. Our tradition is still very new, and we are assigned the task of continuing to develop it to make it better and more comprehensive.

This book was not written for those who feel that the Mystery of initiation is sacrosanct where even the suggestion of changing these rites goes completely against their steadfast adherence to what they believe to be a kind of Witchcraft orthodoxy. They will reject the notion that we should not only examine our initiatory rituals but that we can add additional lore to enhance our experience and advance the practice of modern Witchcraft. For everyone else, this book was written as the final flagstone in the revised and augmented path of modern Witchcraft. Orchestrating the transformative powers and developing insight into psychic transformation is likely one of the most important skills that a Witch or Pagan could adopt since it would give them the ability to function as shamanic witchdoctors, combating the psychic ills of our post-modern world for themselves and their Craft associates.

PART ONE

TRADITIONAL INITIATION

CHAPTER ONE

BRITISH TRADITIONAL WITCHCRAFT— THREE INITIATION ORDEALS

*"The Witches usually know instinctively whether
a person belongs within their coven."*
ALEX SANDERS

Over the many years that I have practiced Witchcraft, I can place a boundary in the timeline of my life indicating the time before I was initiated and the time afterward. Prior to getting my first-degree initiation, I practiced a form of Witchcraft and magic that was based on the meager amount of information available in books at that time. After that event, I was given the training and the source materials to fully function as a Witch.

However, something had changed inside me that allowed me to feel truly connected and aligned with the Goddess and God of Witchcraft. I was no longer on the outside looking in, but on the inside looking out into the world. Initiation had bequeathed to me a membership in a coven of Witches who practiced forms of high magic, but that auspicious event brought me so much more than merely membership.

At the time that I was initiated in 1976, after my twenty-first birthday, joining a coven was the only way to get initiated and receive the training and the spiritual alignment that I had so desired for nearly five years. I was not new to magic and Witchcraft, but with the help of my teachers and coven members, I greatly accelerated my growth and sped up the acquisition and mastery of the coven lore. I was something of a prodigy, and I passed through all three degrees in a period of eighteen months. I believed at the time, and still do, that my quick progress was because my initial alignment to my personal Goddess had been given a powerful gateway into my heart and soul due to my transformative experience that was unleashed during my first-degree initiation.

Alexandrians allowed for that kind of quick progress, or so I have been told, whereas Gardnerians ensure that initiates progress steadfastly through the degrees at a much slower pace. They also don't typically consider the background or previous training that a Candidate for initiation might have already achieved. I know a few Alexandrian third-degree Witches who were forced to start completely over by being initiated from first through the third degree as if they had not been previously initiated so that they might switch their lineage from Alexandrian to Gardnerian. The reason given was that these people had not been initiated in a magic circle by a recognized High Priestess of the Gardnerian tradition. However, I digress, since the topic is about the moment in the event when one becomes an initiated Witch.

Traditional Witchcraft taught that a Candidate for elevation had to undergo three ordeals to be considered a master of their Craft. While the first-degree initiation gave the Candidate full membership in the coven and placed them under the training and protection of the coven leaders and the Deities of the covenstead, it precluded involvement in more advanced magical or sacramental workings. There was lore that was exclusively reserved for the second degree, and still additional lore reserved for the third degree.

The three-initiation system in traditional Witchcraft functioned as a barrier placed on the coven membership to separate individuals with various levels of knowledge and ability. Some Mysteries were established for each of the three degrees, as well as certain magical and theurgic practices. We were told that these different stages and their associated barriers were erected for our safety, but they functioned more as a kind of status symbol for the higher-level initiate. Some members went as far as to demean the first-degree members as lower-class members.

Division of any kind within a coven organization is foolish and wrong-headed. That is my opinion, but it is based on my experience and insights into how a coven should function as a unified body. Why create divisions within a small group that can be a great source of friction between members? It is often the case that if there is a hierarchy in a coven, then the leaders represent the elite, and others attempt to build their status with what is left, creating a pecking order between the levels of initiation. This phenomenon, when it occurs in a coven, represents the importance of status and ego instead of working together to present and experience the Mysteries and the magic of the Witchcraft coven. It starts with the leaders and moves downward from there to the newest members, and it is an unnecessary distraction from the real work.

Initiation as Cultic Entry and Privilege

The questions that need to be asked are: What is the purpose of the three degrees in traditional Witchcraft? What do they represent to the individual who has chosen to undergo them? These degrees, contrary to how they have been used to establish status, represent three levels of the Mysteries that are part of the initiation process. They do not confer any kind of status, but they can confer responsibilities and obligations. Since each member is unique regarding their experiences and the outcomes of these initiations, there should never be any kind of barrier between someone initiated to the first, second, or third degree. Everyone is equal in the eyes of the Deities—they are all the hidden children of the Goddess. Someone might have additional responsibilities or obligations to their coven and community, but everyone should share equally in the Mysteries and magic of the coven.

For the ordeals and Mysteries of the first and second degree, the experience of spiritual death and rebirth are enacted. The first degree represents the transition from an outsider to a full member of the Witchcraft cult. Their old life is sacrificed, and they are given a new name and identity, consecrated, and empowered as a member of the coven. The obligations and responsibilities of the newly born Witch are to maintain the secrets and practices of the Craft, safeguard the coven and its members, and learn to master the rituals of the esbat and the sabbat.

The second degree is similar, except the intensity of the ordeal is amplified three times and the Mystery of Death and Rebirth is enacted as a mystery play in order to teach the reinitiated member that death is never final and that transformation within life, as well as a part of death, is an expected possibility. A second-degree Witch is assigned to

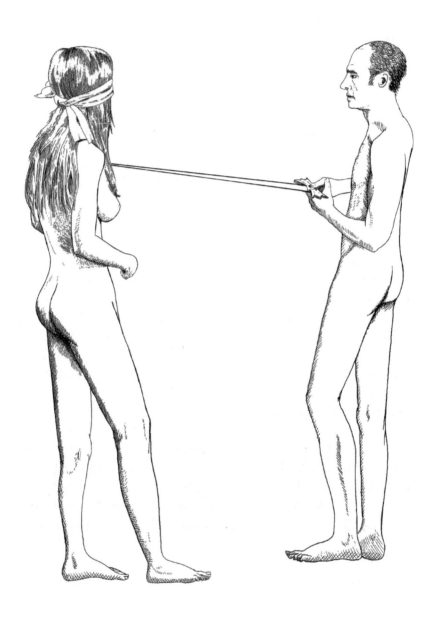

master the secrets behind this mythic mystery play and to assume the obligations and responsibilities of functioning as an initiator of the first degree and as a leader for the rites and practices of a functioning coven.

There are two ordeals in traditional Witchcraft, but there are three degrees. This might seem strange except that the third-degree initiation is not an ordeal. It is a sacramental transition where the Great Rite is performed, and the priestess and priest partaking in this ritual enactment receive the physical and tangible consecration and empowerment of the Craft Deities into their bodies and their souls.

The Great Rite can be performed by the coven leader and the Candidate or by a pair of Candidates who are elevating themselves as future coven leaders. It is customary in British Traditional Witchcraft for the Great Rite to be performed by opposite sex partners, however, in more contemporary inclusive practices, the dichotomy of gender roles is less resolute. The Great Rite can be performed as an ecstatic sexual act between partners, or it can be performed symbolically. Some traditions require that the Great Rite be performed as an explicit sexual act, and some allow for it to be done in either fashion. What it confers is a sacramental transfer of godlike power and an intimate knowledge of the Deities, yet the obligations and responsibilities of this degree are to assume the humble role of the guide and leader and to hold and pass on the lineage to others. The ascendancy is experienced as a temporary event where the individuals are like the Goddess and the God, which should be both an exalted and humbling experience. The sacramental transformation, though, is permanent, and it can be transferred to others using sacramental theurgy, such as godhead assumption and communion.

These three initiations represent the two ordeals and the one sacramental transition that are a part of the traditional Witchcraft practice. To understand how these initiations work and to uncover the symbols of transformation that they contain requires a deeper analysis of these initiations.

While some might consider me an oath breaker for analyzing the three traditional initiations, I believe that because these rites are already part of the common domain, being available in books and online media, I can discuss them in detail without violating my initiation oaths. What took place when I was initiated are my own secrets. The coven members, Deities, and practices of my various covens are confidential. What remains is the lore that can be discussed.

Additionally, the three initiation rites have an origin that is outside of traditional Witchcraft. When G. B. Gardner developed these initiations back in the 1940s, he had access to only two different sources of information. He didn't invent these rituals from his imagination since they contain what is archetypal as an initiation into a secret society or order. What sources Gardner had in his possession were the four degrees of the O.T.O., conferred on him by Aleister Crowley, and he also had the three degrees of Masonry, as written in *Duncan's Ritual of Freemasonry*, first published sometime in the nineteenth century (1866) and available in most libraries.[2] It is the latter source that Gardner used to write up the first and second-degree initiation rites, or the two ordeals.[3] These two initiations in Masonry would be the Entered Apprentice and Fellow Craft rites. We should examine and compare these two initiation rituals to the two initiations in traditional Witchcraft since that is where the structures, themes, and symbols of transformation likely have their origin.[4]

I am claiming that the first two initiations or ordeals of traditional Witchcraft were taken from these Masonic rites, and by going through the details of both, I should be able to present my case as to the origins of these two rituals. Others have made this claim in the past, such as Aidan Kelly, but I wanted to examine them in detail and present that to you, my readers.

One other point that I wanted to make was that in Masonry, there are three ordeals. If the traditional Witchcraft initiations were based on the initiations in Masonry, then would there not be a third ordeal as well? I have puzzled over this omission for many years, and I found it odd that an Initiate passed over any kind of third ordeal and was given a sacramental elevation and powerful

---

2   Duncan, Malcom C., *Duncan's Ritual of Freemasonry*

3   Kelly, Aidan, *Inventing Witchcraft*, p. 70. Kelly stipulates that the Masonic material that Gardner used conformed more to Co-Masonry. Gardner was a member of a Co-Masonry group in New Forest in the 1930s.

4   Ibid., p. 124. Kelly believes that the first-degree initiation rite in Gardnerian Witchcraft more resembles the Golden Dawn Neophyte initiation ritual, although the source for this rite in Gardner's book collection is unknown.

blessing instead. How did someone prove that they were worthy? Wasn't there some kind of test to prove that a second-degree Witch had mastered their responsibilities and obligations to be allowed to enter the sacramental holy of holies? How that transition was determined seemed very subjective or even a form of favoritism to me, even though I passed through it with much expectation and was rewarded for my efforts. I could have been denied that special consideration if my teachers had not been my friends, and I am aware that others have been barred from elevation for obviously petty and personal reasons.

When I analyzed the first two initiations in traditional Witchcraft and compared them to the first two degrees in Masonry, I also used reverse engineering from Masonry to Witchcraft to write up a third ordeal that would fit nicely with the other two. I believe that my analysis of the three initiations in traditional Witchcraft should include this third ordeal as part of what I am seeking to present in this chapter. So, let us examine the initiations in traditional Witchcraft, comparing them to the Masonic initiations and revealing the subtle symbols of transformation.

INITIATION CRITIQUE
AND THE MASONIC CONNECTION

Masonry is a secret society that emerged in the late seventeenth century but has its historical origins in the early eighteenth century. It originally came from Scotland (or so it is presumed) and then spread throughout England, Europe, and the British colonies. Many other secret societies also had their origin in the middle eighteenth century, such as the Bavarian Illuminati and the Egyptian Masonic rites introduced by Cagliostro. In the twentieth century, the Masonic order was hardly a secret society, and it was there, supposedly in 1910, in Ceylon (Sri Lanka), that Gerald Gardner discovered his passion for Mysteries, secret societies, and the practices of magic, both folk-magic and ceremonial magic.[5] It should also be mentioned that Gardner was a member of a Co-Masonry group in the New Forest

---

5   Grand Lodge of British Columbia and Yukon online encyclopedia—https://freemasonry.bcy.ca/biography/esoterica/gardner_g/gardner_g.html

area and that some of his Masonic material for the initiations could have come from that source. However, the Masonic pattern appears to hold true when I compared the two rites together, although the pattern could also be linked to the Golden Dawn Neophyte initiation rite, yet without the dialogue.

Since Gardner had a fetish for nudity, flagellation, and bondage, he incorporated those practices into his Witch cult rites. However, much of these tropes existed in the Masonic initiations of Entered Apprentice and Fellow Craft,[6] although explicit nudity and scourging with a whip were not part of Masonic initiations, they are implied. Gardner added these attributes to his initiations, although there is little evidence that Witches in England practiced nudity in their rites.

In both Masonic rites of initiation, the Candidate is made to strip off their outer garments and shoes and made to wear a garment where their left leg is exposed to the knee and barefoot, their right wears a single slipper, their left arm and breast are naked, but the right is covered. They have a noose loosely placed around their head, with the end dangling free as a cable tow, and they are hoodwinked or wear a blindfold. According to Masonic teachings, the Candidate is divested of all metals, neither naked nor clothed, barefoot nor shod, wearing a rope cable tow, and blindfolded. This state symbolizes that the Candidate is in a threshold type of existence, between beingness and nonbeing, which is the state that presages the beginning of a transformation.

Similarly, a Candidate for the first- and second-degree initiations in Witchcraft is also naked, with their hands tied behind their back with a cord that also circles their neck and extends loosely as a cable tow and secondary cords tied around their right ankle and above their left knee. They are blindfolded, but the theme is that they are willing to undergo the ordeal and their feet are neither bound nor free. The binding represents the spiritual bondage of their life before becoming a Witch, and their blindness represents that they are without light and unable to see their way.

---

6   Duncan, Malcom C., *Duncan's Ritual of Freemasonry*—I have distilled the steps and instructions of the three initiations for Entered Apprentice, Fellow Craft, and Master Mason from this work.

These themes are also the same kind of precursor state of in-betweenness that we see with the Masonic Candidate. It represents that threshold state when a person can no longer proceed as they did previously but are unaware of how they can move forward in their life and in what direction should they proceed. It is a state of complete helplessness and vulnerability, which the Candidate has voluntarily allowed themselves to undergo. When a transformation occurs, it is often not such a voluntary occurrence, as we shall see.

A Candidate is sequestered prior to the initiation in both Witchcraft and Masonry since they are not privileged to observe the Mysteries associated with the workings of the temple and the sacred operations within the magic circle. This occurrence is done for both degrees in both traditions, showing that there is a remarkably similar approach to the methodology for initiation. When the temple is pre-pared in Masonry, for either the Entered Apprentice or Fellow Craft initiation ceremonies, then the Candidate is brought to the threshold for interrogation, vouching, and being declared a proper Candidate. This is also true in Witchcraft, although the circle and temple for a Witchcraft gathering are not differentiated for the elevation, but only members who have passed through that initiation are allowed to participate.

In Masonry, the door to the temple is the threshold of the Mysteries, and it is guarded by a Tyler who is armed with a sword. The door is warded within, and the Candidate is verified and validated by the Junior Deacon and Senior Deacon and receives permission from the Worthy Master to enter the temple. They are brought in and then stopped and challenged by the Senior Deacon with the point of a compass (first degree) or the point of a metal square (second degree) before being allowed to proceed. They are shown to the three cardinal posts where the temple officers reside (the north is not represented) and then brought to the center of the temple where there is an altar with a bible. They kneel with their left leg on the floor, but their right leg forms a square, placing their right hand over the square and compass while their left hand holds open the bible. The members form a ring around the Candidate and make the due-guard sign of the degree. It is in this position that the Candidate is given the oath of fidelity to the order, their brothers, their obligations as an initiate, and the penalty of their obligations, which is a form of throat cutting or disembowelment.

Once the ordeal is past, the blindfold is removed along with the cable tow, and the Candidate is presented with the apron of the degree. They depart from the temple and return fully dressed in their clothes with apron properly tied around their waist, and then are given the instruction of this degree, shown the tools, and most importantly, shown the step, sign, grip, due-guard sign, and the word associated with the degree. The step, sign, grip, and word are the keys to the Masonic initiation, used to acknowledge a brother of the degree when meeting a stranger. This is followed by another transit of the temple where the Candidate is required to show the step, sign, grip, and word with each of the officer positions in the temple and finally, the Master.

In the Fellow Craft initiation, there is a Mystery presentation given that occurs in the secret middle chamber of the temple, ascending the three, five, and seven steps, and being shown the Mysteries of the entrance pillars, the Fellow Craft wages, three jewels, and the mystic letter G and its meanings.

A Witch undergoing both first and second degree is brought into the magic circle from the northeast corner where they stand: naked, partially bound, blindfolded, alone, and unaided. The Initiator approaches them with a sword extended so that the point touches their breast, and they are challenged and urged to prove themself worthy and willing to undergo their ordeal. Showing a willingness, the Initiator gives them a kiss, offers a password, and then brings them into the consecrated circle with the body of their Initiator pushing into the circle and then spinning slowly clockwise to gain entrance into the sacred space. A second-degree initiation might dispense with the challenge, but the Candidate is still blindfolded and partially bound. I have seen second-degree initiations where there is a challenge given to the Candidate at sword point, just like in the first-degree initiation.

Like the Masonic initiation, the Candidate is guided around the magic circle and declared to the four quarters as a Candidate Initiate. (Witchcraft includes the northern cardinal direction.) Also, they are brought to the center of the temple where the members of the coven cluster around them, laying hands upon them as they perform a tight variation of the Witches' dance and draw down the power upon the Candidate. This is where the Candidate is charged and empowered with the energies that were raised in the magic circle prior to their entrance.

Once the Candidate is so empowered, then the Initiator bows before them, gives them the five-fold kiss,[7] then anoints these five points with consecrated oil and consecrated wine. They are declared as an equal (since the Initiator bowed before them) and have now been physically consecrated. The Initiator takes their measure with a thread or thin rope and ties knots in it for the diameter of their head and waist so that it truly and symbolically represents them. The Initiator may keep this measure or return it to the Candidate, depending on the tradition or the despotic tendencies of the coven's leaders.

They are now ready for the ordeal of kneeling, with a sword to their neck, taking an oath of fidelity to the tradition, the coven members, their obligations as a Witch, and the penalties of that obligation (to be self-cursed). Yet, before they take that oath, they are scourged with the coven whip a total of forty times to be purified. Once that is done, then they are helped to rise, unbound and the blindfold removed, and they are embraced by their Initiator and by the members of the coven. They are declared to all the members as a Witch, giving their new name and identity in the coven.

With that task completed, the Candidate is shown the magical tools of the coven and given instruction on how to comport themself within the circle for the time when they return as a full member. They are presented with the three cords that were used to bind them and shown how to wear them as a member of the tradition. Cakes and wine that have already been consecrated are shared with the Initiate as a festive observation and communion with the Goddess and God of the covenstead.

Once these tasks are completed, and before the circle is closed, the Candidate is taken to the four quarters and presented as a new Witch, using their name to identify them to the dread lords of the watchtowers. Typically, after the circle is closed, the coven has a feast in honor of its newest member. This is probably why initiations were

---

7   Five-fold kiss may be taken from the five points of fellowship in the delivery of the sacred word of a Master Mason.

also performed during one of the sabbats, where Candlemas Eve was most traditionally used for initiations.

A second-degree initiation in traditional Witchcraft had a second part to the initiation rite where the mystery play depicting the descent of the Goddess into the underworld domain of death[8] is performed. This is where she meets the Horned God, and by his hand, suffers purification, death, and rebirth (scourging), and through that ordeal discovers her passionate love for him. It is an odd mystery play that has slight overtones of S&M (Sadism and Masochism) and Stockholm Syndrome, but it is the theme of the Mystery of Death and Rebirth, which would be appropriate for a nature-based Mystery religion. I prefer the ancient Sumerian version of this myth, where the Goddess Inanna descends into the underworld ruled by her sister, Ereshkigal, where she undergoes death and rebirth to know the full cycle of mortality and to offer hope and compassion as its antidote.

Additionally, the second degree also has the reversal, where the Initiator trades places with the Candidate to be bound and scourged with three times the strokes given to the Candidate, for 120 in all. This teaches the Candidate how to bind someone who seeks initiation, but it seems to be more of a kind of fetish that would allow the Initiator to receive the attention of the whip and the kiss. I can sense Gardner's urges in these ritual themes, but it does teach the Initiator that to elevate someone to the second degree is a great responsibility, and with it is a certain amount of pain that goes along with the responsibility.

When you compare the Witchcraft initiation ordeals with the Masonic initiations of Entered Apprentice and Fellow Craft, the ritual patterns are very similar. They are, without a doubt, too much alike to be considered a coincidence. While Gardner added nudity, bondage, and flagellation to these Witchcraft initiations, the pattern and stages of the initiations are identical to each other. I believe that we can conclude that Gardner used the two Masonic initiations as his pattern to develop the Witchcraft ordeals.

---

8   This play represents the cycle of the heroine, and it is an unmentioned but important key process.

Missing Third Ordeal

While it can be shown that the first two degrees of the traditional Witchcraft cult were modeled after the Entered Apprentice and Fellow Craft initiations in Masonry, the puzzling thought is why Gardner didn't also develop a third ordeal based on the Master Mason degree. While the third degree in Masonry is quite involved, long, and complex, the pattern is easily derived and could have readily been used to create a third-degree ordeal for traditional Witchcraft. Instead, traditional Witchcraft used a sacramental ritual, the Great Rite, to function as the method for determining the final degree of achievement.

I have previously discussed how the Great Rite was developed from Aleister Crowley's Gnostic Mass, and in fact, passages were directly plagiarized from that mass rite into the Great Rite in the Book of Shadows. While I don't have a problem with that kind of borrowing and it certainly doesn't detract from what the rite is supposed to do, I find it strange that there are only two ordeals in traditional Witchcraft. In my opinion, there should be at least three ordeals, and some years ago, I spent some time developing my own version of that ritual and what it would look like. I will present this ritual, published for the first time, in the next chapter, but in this chapter, I wanted to discuss the corresponding Masonic initiation rite and derive the pattern for the Witchcraft third ordeal initiation rite, as I have done for the previous two.

The overall theme for the three degrees of Masonry has to do with the builders of the great Temple in Jerusalem, undertaken and supervised by the Master Architect and Mason from Tyre, named Hiram Abiff, for King Solomon. The precedence of this story is that it comes from the Bible and incorporates historical characters. The builders are represented by three classes: Apprentice, Fellow Craft, and Master. What is shown in the initiation ceremonies for these three classes are the underlying Mysteries as established by the ultimate Architect and builder of the universe, God himself. While the temple of Jerusalem is the archetype for the initiatory proceedings, the tools and their associated use are symbolic representations of the tools that God used to build the universe. They represent virtues, philosophical aspirations, and higher spiritual values that set apart the initiated Mason from the rest of humanity.

However, the third degree of Master Mason has behind it the terrible murder of the Architect and Master, Hiram Abiff, by three Fellow Craft brothers who illegally sought the Mysteries of a Master. True to his Craft, Hiram had refused each of the three brothers. Because the Master, who was the sole holder of the Mysteries of the Master Mason degree consisting of the grip, sign, and the word—the true knowledge of that degree is tragically lost with the death of Hiram Abiff. The three brothers admit their guilt when they are apprehended and their crime is revealed, and they suffer three different forms of execution. Fellow Craft Masons are sent to the four corners of the known world to rediscover these Mysteries, but they fail. However, a merciful God does reveal to them replacement secrets after much travel, suffering, and time spent without the guidance of the Master's wisdom.

That theme can't be used in a Witchcraft context, of course, so instead, I derived the second half of the Descent of the Goddess myth where she awakens and instills the process of rebirth upon herself and the land. Since without the life-giving powers of the Goddess, all of nature has succumbed to the dormant sleep of winter. However, when the Goddess awakens the life within her and begins her ascent to the lands that she had left, all the dead, sleeping, and dormant attributes of life awaken and walk with her from out of the underworld and into the daylight where life is renewed and reborn. The Horned God is left behind with a broken heart, but then he too realizes that he has a role to play upon the land and makes his exit from the underworld to become the Green Man, God of Verdant Life.

I felt that the theme of the ascent of the Goddess into spring and life from the winter of death was the perfect lesson for the third-degree Witch. So, the second-degree Mystery was to learn of the blessings and preparation that death brings to the hidden children of the Goddess, and the third-degree initiation is a continuation of that Mystery showing that death is but a phase of nature, and that which dies is also reborn in other forms. This perfectly completed the story of the Descent of the Goddess into the underworld, and the third ordeal seemed to complete the ordeals that must be over-come and endured by the thrice-initiated Witch. Once the ordeals are passed, then the third-degree initiation may meet the Deities of Witchcraft through the sacramental rite of the Great Rite.

The basic theme for the third degree, as taken from the ceremony of the Master Mason, has a great surprise for the Candidate who undergoes this initiation. The Candidate is led through the same process of being stripped, half-dressed, barefoot, hoodwinked with cable tow, brought into the temple once proven to be worthy and at the permission of the Worthy Master, and the password given to the Candidate. They are presented to the three stations and transit around the temple three times. They are given a lecture, sometimes parts of which are sung, and then brought before the center altar to swear an even greater oath than previously, with more pressing obligations and penalties should they break that oath. Once sworn, they are freed from the hoodwink and cable tow, and they are shown the three steps, the pass-grip and the real grip, sign, and word of a Master Mason, similarly as they were for the previous two degrees. Once passing this entrance process, they are shown how to wear their apron and then sent to an antechamber to dress. When they return, they are given the jewel and collar of the Junior Warden and presented to the stations of the temple as a Master.

However, even as the officers are seemingly getting ready to end the initiation ceremony, the Candidate is hoodwinked again, accosted by members playing the part of three ruffians who are seeking the grip, sign, and word of a Master, the last of which uses a mallet or maul to assault their head and pushing them onto a canvas bed held steadfastly by members and gently lowered to the floor where they are covered as if a corpse. The mallet or maul is of course padded, and there is no real pain inflicted by these events. They are done to simulate what was done to the Master Mason, Hiram Abiff. Then, while the Candidate lies in their covering as if dead, the mystery play of the murder, capture, judgment, and execution of the three brothers who committed the murder, and the partial restoration of the secrets and Mystery of the Master Mason, are enacted by the members. The Candidate hears it all but cannot see it happening because they are hoodwinked. Once the mystery play is completed, the Candidate is helped to rise and is shown the real grip and word of Master Mason, which consists of the embrace of the five points of fellowship.[9]

To copy the pattern of the initiation ceremony of Master Mason for a Witchcraft presentation, the Initiate will undergo a typical initiation rite made perhaps more serious and severe than what was experienced previously. When it is completed and the Initiate is adorned as a priest or priestess, they are accosted by the priest or priestess who is not the Initiator and accused of being falsely presumptuous and ignorant of the true Mystery of the third degree.

The newly initiated member is blindfolded again with their hands tied in front and helped to lie in the center of the circle. Then, while in this state of silent repose, the Mystery of Rebirth, eternal love is read by the members who sit themselves around the body of the Candidate. Yet it speaks of the sorrowful separation of the Horned God from the Goddess once life is renewed. After the Mystery is read, the key point made that arose from the above world, signifying undying love, is placed into the wine of death and given to the Horned God that he might know and ascend into the world of the living himself (as the Green Man), the Candidate is freed of the blindfold and bindings and given the same sacrament of wine and rose petals to drink, to assist in the Mystery of Rebirth. Then the Candidate joins the coven members sitting in the center of the circle in a silent meditation to fully realize this Mystery, and the circle is closed in the traditional manner.

This third ordeal that I developed is a proper way to complete the initiation ordeals of traditional Witchcraft. While I wrote it and managed to convince a couple of people to reenact it, it was never accepted as part of the creed of my Alexandrian tradition. Of course, the Gardnerians would have rejected it out of hand because it wasn't part of the Book of Shadows canon as written by Gerald Gardner and revised by Doreen Valiente. Still, this extra ordeal fits the pattern of initiations for Blue Lodge Masonry, so I believe that it should have a place of honor amongst Witches. That is why I have presented it here for you to examine, and the actual rite is in the next chapter for

---

9   The five points of fellowship in the Master Mason initiation have similar attributes to the five-fold kiss in traditional Witchcraft. Even the name of practice, as the "Craft" and the use of the phrase "So Mote it Be" are likely taken from Masonry.

you to read in detail. Time will tell whether my idea catches some interest in the Witchcraft community or gets ignored. I am hopeful, but not optimistic.

Since the traditional third-degree initiation is a sacramental rite, it doesn't truly function as an ordeal that must be undergone by the Candidate for that degree. I also consider it to be quite a jump to go from the second degree to the Great Rite, which functions more as an honorific than a true test of worthiness that a third-degree initiatory ordeal would confer. However, that is an issue I leave to the various leaders of the Witchcraft traditions to resolve. I have already discussed in detail the attributes of sacred sexuality in my book *Sacramental Theurgy for Witches,* so I will not discuss it further here.

CHAPTER TWO

THE THIRD ORDEAL INITIATION FOR MODERN WITCHCRAFT

*"It was the teaching of the Wicca that the pathway
of the initiate was to descend into the darkness
of Annwyn (Underworld) beneath the waves to
search for the Grail."*

ALEX SANDERS

The initiation for the third degree was developed and written to fill an apparent gap in the initiatory process and to make certain that the Candidate who receives it is made very much aware of what is expected of them as liturgical leaders and representatives of the lineage and line of initiates. The third-degree Initiate is also completely autonomous, whether the Great Rite is performed or not, and this autonomy must come at a very high and dear price.

Before the Candidate undergoes this third and final ordeal, they must present a completed copy of their Book of Shadows, made in a bound and hard-covered book, beautifully embellished and scripted so that it can be used for a covenstead Book of Shadows. This book is placed on the altar and then incensed and charged by the coven after they raise the power. The Candidate may choose a new name or may keep their second-degree name for this rite. The Candidate also has acquired a Staff of their rank, and this is used in the drawing down of the power.

The High Priestess, the High Priest, and participating third-degree coven members cast the circle and set the Four Wards of Power in the manner of the third degree, using the astrological configuration or some similar method. They then raise a vortex, and within it, a pyramid of power, and invoke the Goddess and the God.

The Candidate for the third degree is led, partially bound and blindfolded before the magic circle as in the first and second degree, and is spun widdershins by the Initiator as they enter it. The Candidate is then brought to the center of the circle. The Initiator takes up their sword and points it at the Candidate's breast as in the first degree, and says:

"Thou art come before us to be weighed and measured, challenged, and judged for the third and final time—but this is the gravest of them all. Who vouches for this Candidate for the third degree?"

MEMBER: *"I vouch for them."*

INITIATOR: *"Are they aware of the gravity of this third ordeal?"*

MEMBER: *"They are and have come to us willing to undergo the ordeal, whether to succeed or fail."*

INITIATOR: *"Then let the ordeal commence, and be of mind, that where success is rebirth and life lived in joy; so, failure is death and utter loss!"*

Then, while the Candidate is still standing before the Initiator, they are asked the following three questions. Failure to answer them wisely will result in the initiation ending here, with the Candidate led in shame and humiliation from the magic circle to a place outside of the circle, there to be coached (by the one who vouched for them) and to meditate. The Candidate may decide then to either return and attempt the ordeal again, or to try the ordeal at another time.

FIRST QUESTION: *"What is the first Mystery that you learned when becoming a Witch?"* [*The passwords are "Perfect Love and Perfect Trust," and they are answered with a kiss, and the Initiate is then pushed into the circle with the body of the Initiator.*]

SECOND QUESTION: *"What is the second Mystery that you learned when undergoing the second ordeal?"* [*The Law of the Threefold Return.*]

Third Question: *"What is the third and greatest Mystery of our faith?"* *[The Great Rite.]*

If the answers are acceptable, the Initiator says:

"Thou hast answered the questions correctly, and now thou shalt undergo the ordeal."

If the answers are not at all forthcoming, then the Initiator shall say:

"Thou dost not know the Mysteries of our faith, and thus thou art judged to be false. Be gone from us and return only when thou dost know the Mysteries!"

Once this trial is completed, the Initiator then presents the Candidate to the four quarters, saying:

"Hear Ye, O Mighty Ones, dread lords of the watchtower of the [cardinal direction], that [Witch's name] is properly prepared to be made a High Priest/High Priestess of the third ordeal."

Then the Candidate is taken to the center of the circle, where their legs and ankles are secured in the traditional manner. The coven members close in around the Candidate to perform the Witches' dance. The power is summoned down upon them in the traditional manner, except the Staff is used, and it is placed behind the Candidate in such a manner so that their bound hands cross over it, with the staff pressed firmly against the back and buttocks. The coven then chants the Witches Rune as they dance step, close in, and draw down the power as was done in the first and second-degree initiations, except that the power travels down the Staff and the spine of the Candidate.

When this task is completed and the Staff is retrieved, the Candidate is assisted to kneel before the altar, and a coven member holds a sword to their neck while the Initiator stands before them and says:

"To attain this highest and most sublime degree it is necessary to suffer and be purified. Art thou willing to be purified?"

33

CANDIDATE: *"I am!"*

INITIATOR: *"I purify thee to take this Great Oath rightly!"*

The postulant is scourged with three hard strokes in all, and the bell is rung three times for each stroke.[10]

Then the Initiator administers the Great Oath. This oath, once given, shall ever free the Candidate from any constraint except by that of the Gods themselves, and so it is given most gravely.

The Initiator says:

"I give thee this terrible oath so that I may free thee of all bonds to me and have thee stand as a guardian and guide of our lineage. Thus, repeat after me:

I [Witch's name], before the Goddess and the God of this covenstead, swear with all my heart and spirit that I will faithfully conduct myself as a guardian and a guide to all who aspire to be admitted to our Witchcraft family. That I will perform the sabbats, esbats, and initiations, as well as all other magical tasks, not only within the letter of the laws and ethics handed down to me by this branch, but most importantly, within the spirit of these laws and ethics, for they are now writ upon my soul. That I will approach changing my ways with the utmost gravity and with all due consideration so that I will behave to all as a steadfast exemplar of my practice and my faith. May the Goddess and God curse and strike me down and make me blind and without any enjoyment in this world, bar me from the other worlds, forever cast me out of the secret cycle of rebirth, and drive me from the Hidden Children if I break my oath and reveal any of the secrets of the Craft except it be to one properly prepared as I am now. Forever and ever unto all eternity! So Mote it Be."

---

10   Ensure that first aid supplies are available after the ritual in case of any broken skin. Observe all basic first aid practices to prevent infection and limit contact with bodily fluids.

Then the Initiator reads the Laws and Ethics so that they are forever remembered.

The Candidate is then assisted to rise to their knees with their head bowed, and the Initiator then stands before them and takes a vial of oil, which is blessed, and then a small amount of it is poured upon the crown. The Initiator says:

"I consecrate thee with oil upon the crown of thy head, so thou art an anointed one amongst the Witches."

Then the Initiator places both of their hands upon the Candidate's head and leans forward, blowing their breath upon the crown of the Candidate's head. The Initiator says:

"From the sacred breath of the Gods, I imbue thee with the powers and authorities of a High Priest/ess of the Craft of the Wise. May you take this gift unto your spirit, and may it wax and grow to greatness within thee. So Mote it Be. Therefore, I welcome thee to the ranks of the elders and leaders of our family!"

The Candidate is assisted to rise to their feet and is unbound and the blindfold is removed. The one who vouched for the Candidate assists with the fastening of the white cord around their waist. They are then assisted to kneel before the Initiator one more time, and the Initiator takes up the future covenstead Book of Shadows and places it in the Candidate's hands, saying:

"Receive this Book of Shadows from the elders of your initiatory line. Know that it contains all that you will need to begin your path as a spiritual leader. But know also that it is never complete and cannot ever reveal any of the Mysteries of our faith. For behold, we are not people of the Book, and the Mysteries cannot be written but only experienced. What is entrusted to you on this night can only aid and guide you, but never direct nor teach you. The ways of the Gods are shadowy and mysterious, and the ways of fate are inexplicable and unalterable! So Mote it Be."

Then the Candidate rises to their feet and is given the Staff by the High Priest/ess, who bows to receive it. The Initiator says:

"Receive this Staff of Authority and Power, and let it be your greatest tool, representing your role as a shepherd to your people. Guide them with love, goodness, compassion, understanding, and insight. Be gentle with the Staff of Authority, and not overbearing, or the Gods may seek thy humbling (for hubris is so hated amongst the Mighty). So Mote it Be."

The Candidate hands the Staff off to the member who vouched for them and then stands in the pentagram position before the Initiator. The Initiator then anoints the eight points of the Sign of the Third Degree and their lips with wine, and then lastly, with oil.[11] The High Priest/ess says:

"I give thee the Sign of the Third Degree, that you might know it, and share it in turn with another member properly prepared as thou art in the Great Rite. For therein, thou shalt come to know the Gods, and begin to learn to live as they do. So Mote it Be."

The Candidate is turned to face the present members, and the Initiator bows before them and says:

"I salute thee now, O Member, Leader, and High Priest/ess of the Witches! Thou hast bravely passed the test and are one amongst us!"

Everyone now applauds and they embrace and kiss, beginning first with the member who vouched for the Candidate. When this joyous occasion is completed, the Initiator presents the moon tiara, moonstone necklace, and cuffs; or the horned crown, horn necklace, and stang depending on whether they are representing the God or

---

11   I will omit describing these eight points (based on the pentagram and triangle). It is something that can be found in other Witchcraft books.

the Goddess. Thus arrayed, the Initiator then escorts the Candidate to the four quarters by the hand, saying the following:

"Hear Ye, Thou Dread Lords of the [direction], that [HP(s) name] has been made a tested and anointed High Priestess/Priest and Magus/Witch Queen of the Goddess!"

Once this is completed, the Initiator and the Candidate proceed to the center of the circle as if to end the rite, when they are approached by the priest or priestess who is armed with their athamé, and approaches the Candidate, pointing the blade at their heart, saying:

"Thou art not one of the anointed ones unless thou hast undergone the third ordeal Mystery! Thou art false and should therefore die!"

Someone comes up behind the Candidate and slips the blindfold over their eyes while another binds their hands with a cord, so they are held together before them. All then assist the Candidate to lay in the center of the circle on their back.

The Initiator then says:

"As the dead, thou shalt learn this Mystery, so that thou shalt come to know the Mystery of Rebirth and complete the tale of the Descent of the Goddess."

[Then the Mystery is read by a Narrator, Guardian, and Lady.]

NARRATOR: *"As ye have been told in the previous ordeal Mystery, the Goddess entered the underworld and the domain of Death and the Dark Lord to know the Mysteries of that place. And therein she received Death's scourge and his cold hand upon her heart. And they lived there and were one, as lovers and as man and wife. But this time of blessedness was short-lived, for the Goddess of the Living cannot forever dwell in the place of death, or otherwise, all would perish in the world and be locked in eternal winter.*

Thus, in the spring, when the snows melted, the earth became warm, and the winter abated; This was all due to the love our Lady felt for the God who was her one true love. And that love warmed the world and released the power of death that locked the land in perpetual night and sleep. But this time of quickening meant that the Lady of Life must leave her Lord to quicken the world and cause it to be reborn with renewed life at the commencement of the vernal equinox. And so, at that time, she departed the domain of the dead, using the necklace that he had given her, the magical Circle of Rebirth, and there was great sadness in the place, and the souls of the dead did weep and wail." [The coven members make weeping and wailing sounds.]

NARRATOR: *"And the Dark Lord mourned greater than anyone but held himself apart and in dignified silence. As time passed, his sorrow became so great that he could not bear it any longer, and so he laid himself down in the center of that domain and seemed to be dead to all. His beloved followers covered his body with a shroud [the Candidate's body is covered with a white cloth], and they sent the guardian of the gate to seek the Lady of Life and tell her that the Dark Lord was like unto stone and that the dead were in peril of being forever lost in his domain. So, the guardian journeyed to the surface and found all the world filled with the joy of life renewed. He found the Lady of the Living within her sacred grove and bowed before her, and with tear-streaked face, he reported to her all that had come to pass in the realm of the dead in her absence."*

GUARDIAN: *"My Lady of Life, Reborn Goddess of the Rose Ankh, have mercy upon us, those who have lost their lives and wait to be reborn. For the Dark Lord has become stricken with grief for the loss of thee and moves no more. Verily, he is more like the dead than we are! I pray to thee, come, and wake him from his deadly trance so that all will be as before, and the dead may be made ready for rebirth."*

LADY: *"My dearest Guardian, I grieve to hear of our loss, but my place is with the living, and if I leave, then winter will descend again, and the world will grow dark before the season sees its fruits and mankind can properly harvest them. I cannot come to revive my Lord because my place is here. I bow my head in sorrow and consternation, but there is nothing that neither fate nor I can do to aid thee. Remember that I do still love thy Lord, who is as dear to me as all life itself."*

GUARDIAN: *"Then come to his aid, so all may be restored, I beg of thee!"*

LADY: *"I cannot, and I must not—for the balance of nature must be maintained no matter the cost. Fate has bound me so!"*

GUARDIAN: *"Then we are lost, and all that die must forever perish from this world. But wait! Have you not a token for his aid, a means of knowing that you love him, and yearn to be together again with him when the seasons change and the bitter winds of autumn descend?"*

LADY: *"I have this flower [she produces a rose], which is a rose—a Mystery of the living and the dead. I shall give this rose as a token of my eternal and undying love for my Lord. Set it in the purest wine and give it to him to drink. Then he will know that I love him still and yearn for our meeting."*

NARRATOR: *"So, the Guardian took the rose beyond the grave into the underworld and placed it therein in a cup of red wine and gave it to his Lord to revive him. [The Guardian pulls back the shroud and holds a cup of wine with a rose placed in it.] The Guardian spoke these words that the Lady of Life taught him, and he said to his Lord ... "*

GUARDIAN: *"My Lady brings to you this life, and her love is like the rose beyond the grave. With this rose and Wine of Life, I bring you back to us revived and with your sorrow unbound. For behold, thy Lady does love thee, and shows this sign to thee."[The Candidate is helped to sit up, has their hands unbound, and they are given the cup and assisted to drink from it.]*

NARRATOR: *"Then the Guardian helped their Lord up and to drink from the cup, and he was restored to his new self, full of life and love. So, he stood up and resumed his place in that dark world, knowing that his Lady truly loved him and would be with him soon." [The*

Candidate is assisted to rise, the blindfold is removed, and they are standing in the center of the circle.]

Narrator: *"But being revived was not enough because the Dark Lord was still alone. For having drunk of the Cup of Life and having gazed upon the rose of her Love, he yearned for her even more. But armed with her cup, which is the Cauldron of Rebirth, he found the way to the gate of the threshold of life and death, and thereby, crossed over into the land of the living, leaving behind the domain of the dead with the promise that he would return to complete his work there. But as he crossed into the world of the living, a great transformation occurred. He changed from the Dark Lord of Shadows to the Lord of Life, the Lord of the Trees, and the Fields, and as the Green Man[12] of Beltain, he went to the Grove of the Lady of Life and therein was united with her in perfect love and trust. And they feasted and celebrated their reunion, all the days, from Beltain until Samhain, when the Lord had to return to the underworld to complete his work. But his Lady returns before him, leaving the world in the autumn equinox, and causing him to mourn and then to pass back into his dark domain; there to be reunited with her once again—to complete the work of rebirth."*

Narrator: *"Thus is the Mystery of the Cycle of Rebirth, and all that it is for life, death, and the continuous cycle. Thus is the Mystery of the Holly King, who is the Dark Lord of the Underworld, and the Oak King, who is the Green Man and Lord of the Trees!"*

Once the narration of this Mystery is completed and the participants wait a short while in meditative silence to plumb the meaning of the Mystery, then the rite is completed. The circle is sealed, and all leave the circle to join in the feasting hall for a great feast—for there is no greater celebration than that of the newly made leader of the Witches.

---

12 He could also have transformed himself into a Roebuck man, the Horned God as a living man-beast.

CHAPTER THREE

NON-TRADITIONAL INITIATIONS— BEYOND THIRD DEGREE

*"For the initiate, there are two types of death: the
death of the body and the death of initiation."*
ALEX SANDERS

In the Alexandrian tradition of Witchcraft, there has often been speculation about initiatory ordeals beyond the third degree. Since the Golden Dawn and the O.T.O. had higher initiations, not to mention the Scottish and York rites of Masonry, a tradition vested in only a three-degree system would somehow be better if it had additional degrees. There would, of course, be greater responsibilities and obligations, as befitting higher degrees and their associated ordeals, but there would be a greater status as well. Of course, there were only three degrees in the standard Book of Shadows, so anything higher would be held in greater confidence and secrecy than the more-known three. Attributions of an ancient provenance for these secret degrees would, of course, be a fabrication. There are allusions to a fourth or higher degree in the Book of Shadows for Alexandrians, but it only exists in the Alexandrian version as far as I know.

The most obvious question would be to ask what possible purpose or function these higher degrees could play in an initiatory system with only three degrees. It would seem to me that undergoing two ordeals and receiving an elevation to the third should suffice to change someone's status from member (Apprentice) to leader (Fellow Craft), to consecrated lineage holder (Master). One could also argue that at least two of these initiations are superfluous and that becoming a member of the tradition should be sufficient. To have more than one degree for admittance to the Mysteries is likely copying the initiatory systems of other social and magical traditions, such as Free Masonry, the Golden Dawn, or the O.T.O instead of determining the necessity of multiple degrees. If you have three degrees, then why stop there? If you cannot justify three degrees from the standpoint of function or role, then one degree should not only be sufficient, but it may be more justifiable from the standpoint of older Witchcraft-based traditions.

Based on my own experiences with magical traditions, lodge organizations, and initiatory ordeals, it would seem to me that there would be a precise function for having five degrees or more. You might ask why five would be a suitable number. This is because purely from a magical perspective, undergoing the ordeals of the four elements and then bringing them together into union for a fifth would follow the basic initiatory process of a magical order. In Free Masonry, such degrees are the Mark Master, Past Master, and Most Excellent Master of the Royal Arch Masonry, which would not be considered in this work because they represent something outside of a magical set of initiations occurring beyond the Master initiation degree. However, the Golden Dawn would come the closest to what we would be considering here, although we should omit the complicated Qabalistic attributes as not having a basis in Witchcraft initiations.

This is how I would group these initiations and establish their function and role if we contemplate a multi-degreed system.

1. FIRST DEGREE—Element Earth: Mastering the foundation of the traditional practice.
2. SECOND DEGREE—Element Air: Mastering the techniques of practical and high magic.
3. THIRD DEGREE—Element Fire: Attainment of leadership, mentoring, and training initiates.
4. FOURTH DEGREE—Element Water: Attaining the consecration of body and soul (Great Rite).
5. FIFTH DEGREE—Element Spirit: Mastering the magic and mystery of the Priesthood of the Mysteries.

A true High Priestess or High Priest of the Craft would be a fifth-degree Initiate and would function much like a prelate in the Catholic church, being responsible for functioning as an intermediator between the Gods and humanity. The other four degrees would represent the important steps or stages along that path. These would be analogous to the five degrees in the Golden Dawn of Zelator, Theoricus, Practicus, Philosophus, and Zelator Adeptus Minor. The fourth degree would be dedicated to establishing a powerful devotional bond with a named Deity just short of full personification, and the fifth degree would represent an ordination given to dispense the sacraments associated with that Deity and all others within the covenstead. The fifth degree would be represented by an inner ordeal or secret chamber of Mysteries, closed to all except to those who have achieved this sublime degree.

This inner order of the Mysteries would have its own triad of initiatory ordeals that would consist of the Grail Fellowship (guardian or knight/maiden of the Grail), coronation of a Witch Queen or King, and the achievement of Hierophant, Master Druid, or mastery of the seven treasures (Mysteries) of the soul. There would be a considerable amount of occult material to build these initiations, as well as the necessity to create and invent lore to build a functioning magical edifice of inner order. I used this perspective to build the degrees of a magical order (Order of the Gnostic Star), but such work would be superfluous to those who would not seek a distinctly magical and liturgical spiritual pathway.

What I have done is to merely show that there are a lot of possibilities available to the ambitious Witch and their equally ambitious coven. I am not the first to travel this path since there was a magical order that had its origin in the mother Alexandrian coven in Boston. Discretion dictates that I do not reveal my sources or details about this order, but I have received it from one of the founders and was informed that this did indeed happen.

I suspect that there have been others as well since the Alexandrian tradition was open to a strictly magical interpretation of the Witchcraft creed. That openness had an impact on what would be considered acceptable practices, organizations, and the development of new or revised occult lore. Unlike the more conservative Gardnerian tradition, the Alexandrians were often compelled to continue the development of their lore since what they received from Gardner was narrow and limited. I believe that this continued research and development was something that Gardner would have approved of since he did so much of it himself.

In this chapter, we should examine the ritual patterns of the higher degrees since they were the kind of rituals that my lineage adherents and I considered to be a regular part of our Witchcraft heritage. We also believed that initiatory degrees should incorporate a magical process and internal struggle or ordeal to perfect and master ourselves. This assumed that a magical initiation would also trigger a powerful internal transformation, becoming the joining of a scripted and unscripted initiation process.

The Fourth Degree Initiation and Ritual Pattern

When a Witch achieves the third-degree initiation, they assume, to some extent, the lineage of their tradition and become de facto spiritual leaders. They can leave the coven of their origin and training and start a new coven. They can also remain in the coven and assist the leadership in elevating the remaining members. We can assume that the Witch has passed through the third-degree ordeal that I presented in the previous chapter, which would make them ideally prepared for the next degree.

The fourth degree is an initiation of devotion and consecration to a specific personalized Deity in the Witchcraft tradition or even the covenstead. This is a form of henotheism that is quite acceptable to anyone who travels a Pagan path since it does not omit the worship of all the Deities. Unlike the previous initiations, it demands a great deal from the Candidate and will take a while to accomplish.

The initiation rite itself then is nothing more or less than a recognition, celebration, and proof that the Candidate has completed the task of achieving a powerful alignment with a specific Goddess or God. They must perform a thorough godhead assumption as part of the rite and prove that the work has been successfully achieved. While the previous three degrees require a subjective assumption on the part of the coven leadership whether a Candidate is ready, and there are a few tests in the second- and third-degree ordeals, the test for the fourth degree is particularly objective to the whole coven. This is because the Candidate has achieved a note-worthy drawing down rite as part of their proof of legitimacy.

The precursor ordeals to taking the fourth degree are that the Candidate has performed the ordeal of godhead personification for at least a lunar phase and functioned as the medium of the chosen godhead in a coven gathering assembled for that purpose. The Candidate has achieved a level of godhead manifestation of a two or even a three, based on the grading of a drawing down rite as judged by coven consensus.[13]

Unlike the previous initiations, the Candidate will perform this initiation rite with at least one to three witnesses who are initiates of the third degree or higher. Following the rite, the Candidate may perform the Great Rite and the Erotic Mass of the Four Goddesses.[14] This is because they have now become a member of the sacramental clergy and have become the medium for the giving of sacralized offerings and blessings.

Magical Mystery Rite for the Fourth Degree Pattern

This rite is performed in a consecrated circle of the Craft, set in the traditional manner. There is a small altar in the center of the circle with a container of consecrated and scented oil.

1. The Candidate stands in the center of the circle, facing east, armed with the dagger.
2. Pyramid of Empowerment: The Candidate proceeds to the eastern watchtower and therein draws an invoking pentagram of Water to the base, then to height, and draws an invoking pentagram of spirit receptive (feminine). Draws a narrow invoking v to connect the two pentagrams, ending with the dagger pointing to the center point between them and exhaling the breath.

---

13 Frater Barrabbas, *Sacramental Theurgy for Witches*, Part One, Chapter Three.
14 Frater Barrabbas, *Sacramental Theurgy for Witches*, Part Two, Chapter Seven.

3. Turns and proceeds to the northern watchtower and performs the same action.

4. Turns and proceeds to the western watchtower and performs the same action.

5. Turns and proceeds to the southern watchtower and performs the same action.

6. Proceeds to the east, turns, and travels to the center of the circle and performs the same action.

7. Returns to the altar, exchanges the dagger for a sword, then proceeds to the eastern watchtower and draws a line from the pylon placed therein to the center of the circle in the zenith, thus connecting them.

8. Proceeds to the north, then the west, and then the south, and performs the same action as in the east.

9. Proceeds to the east and draws a line with the sword from the eastern watchtower to the north, and continues to the west, south, and ending again in the east. The pylon pyramid is now set. Returns to the altar and exchanges the sword for the wand.

10. Proceeds to the east and walks a spiral widdershins circuit toward the center of the circle, passing the east three times. The pyramid vortex is now empowered.

11. Gate of the Mysteries: Stands in the center, facing east, and proceeds to the east, turns, and faces the west. Says out loud:

"I face the three challenges."

12. Draws an invoking spiral to the southeast, envisions the guide, saying:

"My first challenge is to conquer fear."

13. Draws an invoking spiral to the northeast, envisions the guardian, saying:

"My second challenge is to overcome arrogance."

14. Draws an invoking spiral to the west, envisions the gateway of the west and the ordeal, saying:

    "My third challenge is to thwart hubris."

15. Draws an invoking spiral to the zenith in the center of the circle, envisions the fourth way or resolution of the ordeal, saying:

    "The key to overcoming all challenges is the surrender to love."

16. Stands before the west, and proceeds slowly, traveling from the east to the western watchtower, makes the sign of opening the veil of the Mysteries, and steps forward, turns, and feels the light cascading from above the western watchtower to the floor.

17. Proceeds to the center of the circle, imagining walking down a stairway to the darkened underworld. In the center, turn to face the west. Stand and meditate for a brief period of time.

18. Cycle of Light and Darkness, Life and Death: Still holding the wand, proceeds to the north, bows, and draws an invoking pentagram of Earth, saying:

    "Birth unfolds into youth, a time of growing and learning."

19. Proceeds across the circle to the south, bows, and draws an invoking pentagram of Fire, saying:

    "Youth becomes beauty and filled with desire, as the lustful lovers."

20. Proceeds widdershins to the east, bows, and draws an invoking pentagram of Air, saying:

    "Desire is manifested as children, and life passes into parenthood."

21. Proceeds across the circle to the west, bows, and draws an invoking pentagram of Water, saying:

"Desire becomes cold, life brittle, but the heart is full of wisdom. So it shall be until death."

22. Proceeds to the center of the circle, facing the east. Draws in the nadir an invoking pentagram of spirit creative (masculine), saying:

"From birth to death, the continuous cycle of light and darkness, guided through each state by the hand of the All-Father, who symbolizes the ever-changing spirit of mortal existence."

23. Proceeds to the center of the circle where a small altar is placed with a bottle of consecrated oil, deposits the wand on the altar, and then kneels, hands placed open upon it. The Witness proceeds to the other side of the altar, takes up the bottle of oil, and uses it to lightly anoint the hands and forehead of the Candidate. They then step behind and place their hands upon the head of the Candidate, saying:

"In the name of [personified godhead] who you have faithfully served and acted through, I consecrate you and make your body into a temple of that Deity. May you ever guard, preserve, and sanctify this most holy place. So Mote it Be."

24. Then the Candidate recites their dedication to the personified godhead, vowing to serve that Deity and to be always a proper representative.
25. The Candidate and Witness sit in meditation for a period, absorbing all that has occurred within the chamber of the Mysteries. Once this is complete, the Candidate takes up the wand, the altar is taken away, the Witness stands to the side, and the Candidate continues the rite, facing the west and making the sign of the closing of the veil.

26. Proceeds to the western watchtower, turns, and faces the east, saying:

   "I face the three virtues of my Craft and vow to practice them."

27. Draws an invoking spiral to the northwest, envisions the guide, saying:

   "My first virtue is to be charitable to my fellow members of the Craft."

28. Draws an invoking spiral to the southwest, envisions the guardian, saying:

   "My second virtue is empathy, so I will seek to understand the point of view of my fellow members of the Craft."

29. Draws an invoking spiral to the east, envisions the gateway of the east and the ordeal, saying:

   "My third virtue is consensus, so I will seek to know the various opinions of my fellow members and discover a united direction for our clan."

30. Draws an invoking spiral to the zenith in the center of the circle, envisions the fourth way or resolution of the ordeal, saying:

   "May I learn to give these virtues from myself to all human-kind, and thereby achieve wisdom."

31. Stands before the east, and proceeds slowly, traveling from the west to the eastern watchtower, makes the sign of opening the second veil of the Mysteries, and steps forward, turns, and feels the light cascading from above the eastern watchtower to the floor.

32. Proceeds to the center of the circle, imagining walking up a stairway to a brilliant sunrise. In the center, turns to

face the east. Stands and meditates for a brief period. The
ordeal is completed.

33. Draws a sealing spiral each to the four watchtowers, the
zenith, and nadir.

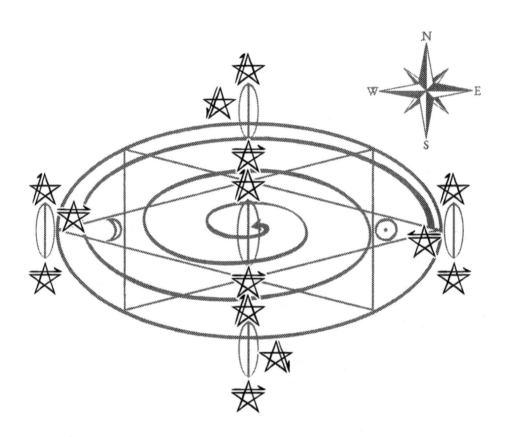

Diagram of the Mystery of the Fourth Degree Rite

The Fifth Degree Initiation and Ritual Pattern

A fifth degree would symbolize the merging of the four element degrees into a fifth, which would be their quintessence and symbolized by Spirit. The fifth degree would also represent a passage from the material world and its concerns to an inner world of Spirit and the source of the ever-changing Mysteries. This initiatory domain represents a kind of inner order where the Mysteries of light and darkness have their origin—the source of eternal renewal.

The nature of this source is inexplicable and ever-shrouded in mystery, but in its material form, it is perceived as the continual cycle of light and darkness, life and death, and rebirth. These cycles are to be found in both the passing of the seasons of the sun, waxing and waning of the moon, birth, death, and rebirth of all living things, and the process of transformative change within the human psyche that emulates all these changes. These inner Mysteries then are the very essence of the process of transforming the human psyche and transcending the barrier between humanity and divinity.

What the fifth degree represents is an inner order of the Mysteries where a suitable candidate receives an office in the preservation and dissemination of their powers and wisdom. Since the Deities are also a part of this eternal dance, then the source of this Mystery is beyond even them. It represents an unchanging and unchangeable source of all things, including the domain of Deities, where all manifestation proceeds at the beginning of time and all manifestation dissolves into it at the end, only to begin the cycle once again. Perhaps the best way to define this Mystery is to call it what the Hindus (Darshan), Chinese (Tao), and Japanese (Do) called it, the *Eternal Way*.

Officers of this inner order consist of Guardian, Priest/Priestess, Sacred Monarch, and Hierophant of the Mysteries. These offices represent the three stages of internal initiation that a fifth-degree Witch would undergo, where Guardian and Priest/Priestess would be a single level with two attributes. One progresses through the fifth-degree stages as one would progress through life, achieving the highest level only after a lifetime of work. Since membership is kept confidential, any outward sign of the three stages is omitted from normal community interaction. If these Mysteries are inexplicable, then any achievement through them is also incapable of being shown to those who are outside.

Features of the inner order temple of the Mysteries are that it has an inner magic circle or consecrated boundary, an altar, a throne, and a pillar (Herm) or an artifact symbolizing the abstract representation of the unnamed Mystery. The conferring of status within the inner order occurs through the recognition by other members of that order, whether in the same clan or coven or even within other traditions. It is given through anointing, laying of hands to the crown of the head, receiving the sacred kiss, and being conferred upon the status of office through the receipt of a triple consecrated tool, such as the sword, stole, scepter, crown, staff, and ring. This consecration is performed by at least one member of the inner order, but through the consideration of at least three before it can be given.

How someone might work toward achieving a fifth-degree initiation is much like the work to achieve the fourth degree. The ordeal is the work that must be done before the initiation rite is performed by the Candidate with the attendance of one or more witnesses. Based on the accomplishments of the previous four degrees, the Candidate must show mastery of the three magical methodologies of energy, mind, and spirit, being the technologies of elemental magic, planetary and talismanic magic, and spirit conjuration through the artifice of a familiar spirit. In addition, the Candidate must have completed a full three-month regimen of godhead personification as a deepening service to a specific Deity and then demonstrated that ability in a gathering of clans. It would also be necessary for the Candidate to have functioned for a while as a priestess or priest and to have trained and initiated others into the Craft. This would represent a very seasoned, experienced, and knowledgeable elder to be elevated into the rank of mistress or master of the Mysteries.

Here is the ritual pattern for the fifth degree, to be performed, of course, by the Candidate and witnessed by one or more members of the inner order of the Craft. If such specific individuals are not available (or don't exist in one's community), then a surrogate witness who is an esteemed elder of the community may act as a proper representative. The inner order Mystery conferring the office of the Mysteries will be discussed separately in the sections below.

Magical Mystery Rite for the Fifth Degree Pattern

This rite is performed in a consecrated circle of the Craft, set in the traditional manner. There is a small altar in the center of the circle with a container of consecrated and scented oil.

1. The Candidate stands in the center of the circle, facing east, armed with the dagger.
2. Pyramid of Empowerment: The Candidate proceeds to the eastern watchtower and therein draws an invoking pentagram of spirit receptive (feminine) to the base, then to height, draws an invoking pentagram of spirit creative (masculine). Draws a narrow invoking spiral to connect the two pentagrams, ending with the dagger pointing to the center point between them and exhaling the breath.
3. Turns and proceeds to the northern watchtower and performs the same action.
4. Turns and proceeds to the western watchtower and performs the same action.
5. Turns and proceeds to the southern watchtower and performs the same action.
6. Proceeds to the east, turns, and travels to the center of the circle and performs the same action.
7. Returns to the altar, exchanges the dagger for a sword, then proceeds to the eastern watchtower and draws a line from the pylon placed therein to the center of the circle in the zenith, thus connecting them.
8. Proceeds to the north, then the west, and then the south, and performs the same action as in the east.

9. Proceeds to the east and draws a line with the sword from the eastern watchtower to the north, and continues to the west, south, and ending again in the east. The pylon pyramid is now set. Returns to the altar and exchanges the sword with the wand.

10. Proceeds to the east and walks a spiral widdershins circuit toward the center of the circle, passing the east three times. The pyramid vortex is now empowered.

11. Gate of the Mysteries: Stands in the center, facing east, and proceeds to the east, turns, and faces the west. Says out loud:

"I face the three pathways of the Mysteries."

12. Draws a rose-ankh to the southeast, envisions the guide, saying:

"My first challenge is to fully know the Mysteries."

13. Draws a rose-ankh to the northeast, envisions the guardian, saying:

"My second challenge is to persevere regardless of limitation."

14. Draws a rose-ankh to the west and envisions the gateway of the west and the ordeal, saying:

"My third challenge is to courageously face all obstacles, especially myself."

15. Draws a rose-ankh to the zenith in the center of the circle, envisions the fourth way or resolution of the ordeal, saying:

"The way of the Mysteries cannot be told. Thus, I shall learn to be silent to hear."

16. Stands before the west, and proceeds slowly, traveling from the east to the western watchtower, makes the sign of opening the veil of the Mysteries, and steps forward, turns, and feels the light cascading from above the western watchtower to the floor.

17. Proceeds to the center of the circle, imagining walking down a stairway to the darkened underworld. In the center, turn to face the west. Stand and meditate for a short period of time.

18. The Cycle of Light and Darkness, the cosmogonic cycle: Still holding the wand, proceeds to the north, bows, and draws an invoking pentagram of Earth, saying:

"The uncreated One moves and, therefore, before it appears its reflection, the birth as manifestation."

19. Proceeds across the circle to the south, bows, and draws an invoking pentagram of Fire, saying:

"Primal Order is manifested, representing the perfection of forms."

20. Proceeds widdershins to the east, bows, and draws an invoking pentagram of Air, saying:

"Imperfection, as a part of Primal Order, causes the endless cycle of birth and death, the ever-turning wheel of light and darkness."

21. Proceeds across the circle to the west, bows, and draws an invoking pentagram of Water, saying:

"All things of energy and matter must ultimately end, and so the dissolution of creation into the uncreated must eventually occur."

22. Proceeds to the center of the circle, facing the east. Draws in the nadir an invoking pentagram of spirit receptive (feminine), saying:

"From creation to dissolution, the continuous cycle of light and darkness generated from the uncreated source All-Mother, who symbolizes the changeless spirit of the eternal source."

23. Proceeds to the center of the circle where a small altar is placed with a bottle of consecrated oil, deposits the wand on the altar, and then kneels, hands placed open upon it. The Witness proceeds to the other side of the altar, takes up the bottle of oil, and uses it to lightly anoint the hands and forehead of the Candidate. The Witness then steps behind and places their hands on the head of the Candidate, saying:

"In the name of [personified godhead] of the outer Mysteries whose servant you are, I consecrate you and bring you into the domain of the inner Mysteries. May you ever guard, preserve, and sanctify this most holy place. So Mote it Be."

24. Then the Candidate recites their dedication to the unnamed Mysteries as a servant of a named Deity, vowing to serve as a holder and representative of those Mysteries and to seek an ever-greater understanding and emulation of them in life and beyond.

25. The Candidate and Witness perform the Inner Mystery Office of the Guardian, Priestess/Priest, Monarch, or Hierophant. Once this is complete, the Candidate takes up the wand, the altar is taken away, the Witness stands to the side, and the Candidate continues the rite, facing the west and making the sign of the closing of the veil.

26. Proceeds to the western watchtower, turns, and faces the east, saying:

"I face the three virtues of leadership and vow to practice them."

27. Draws an invoking spiral to the northwest, envisions the guide, saying:

    "My first virtue is to be adaptable, knowing my own limitations."

28. Draws an invoking spiral to the southwest, envisions the guardian, saying:

    "My second virtue is compassion, to be practiced on everyone equally."

29. Draws an invoking spiral to the east, envisions the gateway of the east and the ordeal, saying:

    "My third virtue is to be authentic, acting as a truthful and humble representative of the Mysteries."

30. Draws an invoking spiral to the zenith in the center of the circle, envisions the fourth way or resolution of the ordeal, saying:

    "May I master these virtues and become a leader representing those Mysteries which can never be told but only experienced."

31. Stands before the east, and proceeds slowly, traveling from the west to the eastern watchtower, makes the sign of opening the second veil of the Mysteries, and steps forward, turns, and feels the light cascading from above the eastern watchtower to the floor.

32. Proceeds to the center of the circle, imagining walking up a stairway to a brilliant sunrise. In the center, turn to face the east. Stand and meditate for a brief period. The ordeal is completed.

33. Draw a sealing spiral, each to the four watchtowers, the zenith, and nadir.

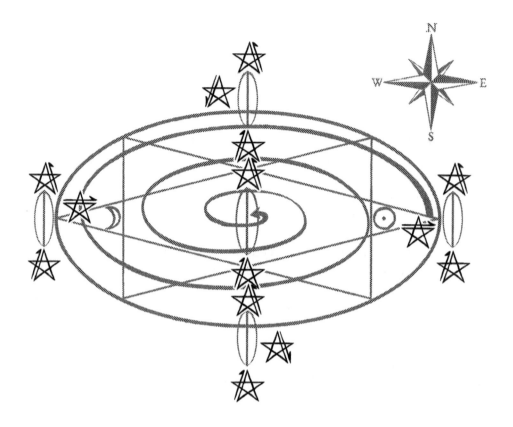

Diagram of the Mystery of the Fifth Degree Rite

What follows are the four Mystery offices that are conferred on the Candidate who has achieved that level of development in the inner Mysteries of the Craft.

Guardian and Priest/ess
of the Mysteries

These two offices are conferred, one after the other, when a Candidate has achieved the fifth degree. They represent the basic operation of a fifth-degree initiate, and the next two offices above these two might be considered very rare or even unattainable. The first office is that of Guardian of the Mysteries since that is a position implicit with obtaining entrance to the sacred Mysteries. Once one is granted entrance, then the obligation to protect and ward these Mysteries from the profane or ignorant becomes a mandatory practice. In other faiths, such as Christianity, this office would have been like the knight warrior who would have protected pilgrims in the holy land, such as the Templars. However, since the Mysteries are inexplicable, and since the temple of the Mysteries for the inner order is symbolic and temporary, there isn't any location that one would physically protect with sword, helm, and shield, nor are the Mysteries knowable except through personal experience.

What the guardian protects is the proper access, the method of experience, and an interpretation of what is experienced. They also ensure the confidentiality of proceedings and the membership of the inner order and can act as the arbiter and judge within the community at large. The tool and emblem of the guardian is a thrice-consecrated sword and sheath, along with a belt to fasten it to one's waist—but it is symbolic of the office and not be used to cause harm or bloodshed.

A priestess or priest (prelate) of the Mysteries represents a fifth-degree Initiate who acts as the mediator or mediatrix of the Mysteries. This office represents the true stage of spiritual leadership, granting the means to discharge the sacraments as an official representing both a specific Deity and the overriding Mysteries to which that godhead resides. A prelate is expected to have a license to perform legal weddings, act as the officiant for naming rituals, requiem rites, and the conferring of the third through fifth degrees. They can also perform the special rites of godhead personification and the mass and benediction rites if those are part of the vested tradition. A prelate, like the guardian, is the outer face of the inner order. The emblem of this office is the stole, worn around the shoulders, representing the yoke of responsibilities that they assume.

Presented here are the simple rites for these two offices. Individuals can make them more elaborate or keep them simple as they are defined here.

Induction to the Office of Guardian Ritual Pattern

1. The Candidate, dressed in a white robe, lays prostrate before the center altar where a thrice-consecrated sword of their choosing is placed. The Officiant asperges their body with lustral water, and then assists them to arise, kneeling three paces before the altar.
2. The Officiant takes the consecrated oil from a bottle on the central altar and anoints the Candidate upon the forehead.
3. The Officiant slides the sword from its sheath and takes it, standing in front of the Candidate, and touches their left shoulder with the tip of the blade, moves the blade over the head, and rests it on the right shoulder while the Candidate bows their head. The Officiant says:

    "In the name of the Great Mysteries that cannot be told, and through your service to [personified godhead], I give you the right to bear this sacred sword to guard this sacred domain."

4. Then the sword is removed from the right shoulder and taken and returned to the sheath. The Officiant then presents the sword, sheath, and belt to the arms of the Candidate and kisses them on each cheek. The Officiant says:

    "Arise O guardian and take up thy holy sword to protect the Mysteries from the ignorant and profane."

5. The Candidate stands before the Officiant and dons the belt and sheathed sword.

Induction to the Office of
Priest/ess of the Mysteries Ritual Pattern

1. The Candidate, dressed in a white robe, kneels two paces before the center altar where the thrice-consecrated stole of their choosing is placed. The Officiant gives communion of consecrated wine and bread to the Candidate.
2. The Officiant takes consecrated oil from a bottle on the central altar and anoints the Candidate upon the forehead and fingers of both hands.
3. The Officiant takes up the stole and places it over the Candidate's head to rest on their shoulders, while the Candidate bows their head. Officiant says:

    "In the name of the Great Mysteries that cannot be told, and through your service to [personified godhead], I give you the right to act as a mediatrix/mediator of the powers and authority of this sacred domain."

4. The Officiant then takes their hands and places them on the Candidate's head, bows low, and blows their breath onto the Candidate's scalp, saying:

    "I will my powers and authority into you, symbolically granting to you the provenance of the ancient lineage of clerics. May you grow to master the Mysteries that cannot be told."

5. The Officiant then kisses the Candidate on each cheek, then says:

    "Arise, O Priest/ess of the Mysteries!"

6. The Candidate stands before the Officiant and assumes the posture of the tau cross with arms extended while the Officiant bows before them.

Monarch of the Mysteries

There is a tradition of making Kings and Queens of the Witches, although that tradition has its detractors, and many do not follow it. Alex Sanders was declared King of the Witches in 1965, much to the chagrin of other traditions of Witchcraft who neither acknowledged that achievement nor considered him worthy of such a claim. In the U.S., there is a tradition of making Witch Queens from a High Priestess in the Gardnerian tradition, particularly one who has functioned as the teacher and benefactor of covens hiving off from her coven. Such a status is marked by a garter worn around the leg, having a buckle for each coven she has officially spawned. This tradition of *queening,* as it is called, is very popular amongst certain Gardnerians in the U.S., but it is almost unheard of by Gardnerians in the U.K. Thus, queening has a limited appeal and is not universally accepted as a traditional initiation rite.

However, within the inner order of Mysteries, there is an office and a role for a Monarch of the Mysteries. What this entails is like the occult mythos of Arthur, who was a monarch spiritually and magically bonded to the very land he ruled. It is why he couldn't die at the hands of his son and became the once and future King of England. A Monarch of the Mysteries is a person who is bonded to the domain of the Mysteries and becomes an advocate and spokesperson or mediator for the sacred and holy earth, that mythic domain that acts as a symbolic representation of the local geographic place. What happens to the land affects everything in that mythic domain, and what happens in that mythic domain has an impact on the local geography. The mythic domain has many names throughout the world, such the fairyland, dream time, elf-land, Kingdom of Heaven, Camelot, Utopia, and many other names.

Creating a bond between a fifth-degree Initiate and the mythic domain of the Mysteries entails a terrible responsibility for the ecological condition of the local geography since the mythic domain is based on that local place where the Initiate might live. Not only must a Monarch of the Mysteries be a channel for the material blessings of the source of the Mysteries and its timeless domain, but they must also take upon themself a kind of stewardship or public conscience for the local area where that monarch resides. It is a very stressful and difficult position to occupy, and due to the short lifetime of a human being, it is a role that has a limited duration. It would not be conceivable that a Monarch of the Mysteries would abdicate their responsibilities after assuming that role for a decade or two. This is because when the land suffers, so will the mystical monarch who acts as the spiritual and magical sovereign.

What, you might ask, are the benefits of undertaking such a role? While it would be highly stressful to occupy this position— and fraught with danger as mindless and soulless corporations and interested parties despoil the environment—it would also give the monarch an incredible insight into the relationship between spirit and matter, and the ability to perform incredible healings, peerless divination, insightful dowsing, and amazing agricultural abilities. Such a person would be able to dispense the wealth of the natural resources, but only if it is performed as a service to others. A Monarch of the Mysteries cannot receive any gain from their loaded powers and abilities, and there are limitations as far as healings are concerned. They must also keep the source of their powers secret and not reveal to the public that they are an Initiate of the inner order of the Mysteries.

Here is the basic rite for a magical and mystical coronation. This rite can be greatly embellished so that it is more like an actual mundane coronation, taking from either the Catholic or the Anglican Christian traditions. I prefer to keep this ritual simple and basic since the objective represents the far more difficult and complex actions of union with the earth. In addition to the central altar, there is also a throne, which is a chair fully draped with a purple cloth. On the altar is a thrice-consecrated crown and scepter, and sacraments of oil, wine, and bread. The Officiant is a Hierophant or a well-respected elder of the community. The rite of this office is attended only by those who have a vested interest in the proceedings, such as the local members of the inner order, if any.

Mystical and Magical
Coronation Ritual Pattern

1. The Candidate as Regent, dressed in a red robe, is wearing a belted sword and the stole of the first two offices of the Mysteries. They are kneeling two steps before the central altar.
2. The Officiant is dressed in a green robe and ivy wreath, holding a staff of the Hierophant, and assisted in this office by an acolyte dressed in a blue robe, stands before the kneeling Regent. The acolyte holds the staff while the Officiant performs their duties.
3. The Officiant gives communion of consecrated wine and bread to the Regent.
4. The Officiant then takes the bottle of oil and pours a few drops upon the head and smears the forehead of the Regent, then takes and lays theirs upon the head of the Regent and breathes their power into them, saying:

    "I consecrate and anoint your head in the manner of the Kings and Queens of the Mysteries, so that you might be placed above humankind and closer to the Gods."

5. The Officiant backs away from the kneeling Regent and bids them to rise, holding their staff of office, while the acolyte assists the Regent to arise. Then the Officiant and acolyte escort the Regent to the throne and assist them in sitting upon it, arranging robes and their sword to be most comfortable.
6. The acolyte holds the staff standing before the Regent as the Officiant takes the bottle of oil from the central altar and dabs some oil on the Regent's naked feet. They then bow and kiss the Regent's feet, saying:

    "You shall grow roots and join with the earth in eternal embrace."

7. The Officiant then rises and takes the crown from the central altar and stands before the Regent seated

on the throne. Holding the crown over their head, the Officiant says:

"In the name of the Great Mysteries that cannot be told, and through your service to [personified godhead], I give you the right to act as a sovereign of the powers and authority of this sacred domain."

8. The Officiant slowly lowers the crown upon the Regent's head.
9. The Officiant then takes the scepter from the central altar and presents it to the Regent, who accepts it with their right hand. The Officiant then says:

"I give you the sacred scepter that acts as the bridge between the domain of the Mysteries and your own terrestrial kingdom. Use it with great care and wisdom, and the Mysteries will aid you in all of your endeavors."

10. The Officiant then leans forward, kisses the Regent on each cheek, and bows low before them.
11. The Officiant takes up the staff and stands with arms held outward with the staff in the right hand and says:

"I have consecrated you as Regent of the Mysteries and Liege of the Earth. In your chosen name, I crown you [Regnant Name], Monarch of the Mysteries of Earth! May you reign in peace and prosperity, forever."

12. The Officiant and acolyte bow low before their sovereign and back away from the throne, returning to the altar. The newly crowned Monarch of the Mysteries sits in quiet contemplation for a time before finally rising and departing. They hand the crown and scepter to the Officiant to hold in safekeeping.
13. At some time later, the sovereign should perform a private handfasting and the Great Rite with a priest/ess who acts as the material representative of the land over which they have become sovereign.

Hierophant Master of the Mysteries

There is no actual office for the Hierophant of the Mysteries since it is an exalted role that has few if any peers. There is no one to either witness this induction or anyone to confer upon the Candidate the recognition required. Thus, this rite would be self-chosen and self-determined, although hopefully not for egotistic purposes.

What is required for one to be a Hierophant is to fully master all the Mysteries of light and darkness, life, and death. Since a person would need to experience a near-death circumstance in life to claim mastery of the Mystery of death, it would be difficult for most to be able to make this claim without deception or falsehood. Also, unless one were medically declared dead and then resuscitated, it couldn't be determined that someone had mastered the Mysteries of both life and death.

These complexities and obvious requirements make the honor of being declared a Hierophant of the Mysteries beyond the ability of nearly everyone. However, the role itself has a powerful and mythic quality that would allow it to be experienced as a transcendent being beyond all life and death, but fully representing both. This means that a Hierophant of the Mysteries exists as an archetypal personage who can be contacted and appear when summoned by any member of the inner order, provided their need for consolation is great and valid.

Like any demigod, the Hierophant or Master of the Mysteries will have a public name and persona and a secret name and image or signature. In the Mysteries that I engaged in when gaining my early initiatory grades, I was told about this secret personage, and that they were the patron of all Witches and Pagans. Some called this secret personage Merlin, others Ambrosius (such as in our tradition), and still others used the names Apollonius or Hermes-Thoth Thrice Greatest. They are the great ancient mage and sage of the Mysteries and working with them for a period will grant the seeker their true and secret name, known only to the initiates of the inner order. When I called upon this majestic being for myself, I experienced their presence as a woman.

A Hierophant of the Mysteries is also like the holy order of the Bishop of the Catholic church, representing a kind of seventh-degree or master of the seven virtues as opposed to the seven deadly sins. A bishop wears a miter and holds a crosier, while a Hierophant wears an ivy wreath and holds a green staff with leaves sprouting from it. What they have in common is they both wear a ring as an emblem of their bond with the Mysteries, and they have two keys that unlock the powers and authorities in both this world and the domain of the Mysteries. A bishop and a Hierophant are fully consecrated, which signifies that they are not fully of this world, being a master of the bridge between worlds, and commanding both terrestrial and celestial or heavenly powers.

Still, while there are many bishops, archbishops, cardinals, and a pope (father) in the Catholic church, the Hierophant of the Mysteries remains mostly a powerful spiritual being who, unlike the Catholic hierarchy, has also mastered the Mysteries of death as well as life. In such a manner, they are more like the mythical Christ than like the bishops of the Catholic church.

CHAPTER FOUR

ESSENTIAL ATTRIBUTES
OF INITIATION

*"An initiation creates a strong emotional bond
and a deep astral tie between coven members, so
consider very carefully who you initiate."*

STAR HAWK

We have covered the traditional three initiation rites based on Gardnerian Witchcraft and its offshoots, and we have examined potential initiation rites beyond the third-degree initiation, which would be more a kind of magical than a cultic initiation. However, what we need to examine is what I would call the most essential attributes of initiation or essential elements that help people make the transition from a secular identity to one that is identifiably a Witch. Do we need to join a coven and undergo their scripted initiation to be made a practicing Witch? Can we practice Witchcraft without having to bond ourselves to a group and take on all that group's issues, politics, and personal baggage?

When I first started my Witchcraft path, I practiced for five years before I finally discovered a coven nearby that would initiate me into the Craft. While that experience greatly accelerated my psychic growth, magical ability, and the depth of my occult knowledge, the group itself was slowly starting to degrade, and after a few years, imploded. It began as the dream coven that I had always wanted to discover and belong to, but over time, it corrupted and fell to become the veritable coven from Hell. A good part of my biography is based on that terrible adventure, and the two leaders of that group became fundamentalist Christians, such was the blowback from that event.

There were two covens in that group functioning in the city of Milwaukee; one was a closed senior coven, and the other was a training coven. However, the two groups contracted to become a single coven, and then further fell apart a few years later. My fellow coven mates who managed to escape that group unimpaired thought that it had been like the epic failure of the mythic Camelot without any redemption, but plenty of painful lessons learned. I felt burned and betrayed by that failure and placed the blame squarely on the High Priest and High Priestess, but we all played an odious part in that epic fall. Subsequent attempts at forming a properly run coven, both shortly after that experience and even years later, showed me the inherent weakness and flaws in the traditional model of the Witchcraft coven. That model relied too heavily on the leaders and gave too little to the members. If a coven had good leaders, then it could survive for a period, but only if authority was shared amongst the members of the group instead of conferred on just the leaders.

Now, four decades later, I cannot in good conscience say that joining a coven and receiving a traditional initiation is the *only* way that a person can become a Witch. I feel that anyone who desires a traditional path to becoming a Witch should be extremely cautious and open-minded, scrutinizing the group dynamics and the leadership of a coven before electing to join. I have the psychic scars to show that capriciously joining a coven without first carefully screening the leaders and the members, and taking time to do that research, can often result in having a bad experience. Covens are supposed to be semi-permanent organizations functioning as beacons of teaching, practice, and camaraderie in their communities, but they are all too often short-lived dysfunctional groups based on ego trips and subjugation rather than an egalitarian social ethos. They are only as good and solid as the leaders and the relationship between them and the senior and junior members.

What I am not saying is that all covens are dysfunctional organizations. There are certainly many successful covens and groups in the various Witchcraft and Pagan communities. Yet the successful ones have one thing in common—they share the responsibility of leading the group and ensuring that decision-making is done in a fair and democratic manner. One coven that I know about has been around for over thirty years and even rotates its leadership, allowing all members to assume the roles of responsibility at some point, but the group operates on consensus. Still, groups that are egalitarian, consensus-driven, and have rotating positions of responsibility are the ideal kind of group; one that is adaptable enough to change and strong enough to retain its identity. These kinds of organizations are built to last many years, even decades.

If you are searching for a traditional coven to receive the typical training, initiation, and elevation, then I would recommend that you carefully look around and take time to find a group whose internal culture fits your personality and has the attributes of a good organization. There is no hurry and there is no need to impulsively join a group that you might later regret having joined at all. However, there is no requirement these days to undergo a traditional initiation to consider yourself a Witch. There are far more resources available to a seeker today than there were when I was first starting my path. Additionally, there is far less of a stigma applied to someone who is not initiated into a traditional path. You will always find someone who smugly derides those who don't have the right kind of lineage or pedigree, but they have become an irrelevant minority in the various communities today.

So, the question remains: How do you become a Witch and what are the requirements? Since this is not a book for beginners, the answer to this question becomes more complex, but it can be reduced to some basic concepts. I will assume that this question has bedeviled some of the more senior members of our community when confronting the arguments of the younger generation who have decided to seek their own independent path in learning and mastering Witchcraft. I know that it puzzled me when I was first asked that question by a young woman who already considered herself a Witch after a fashion.

These basic concepts start out quite simple, but ultimately become quite evolved. It begins when a person declares publicly that they are a Witch. Before that moment, it is being internally processed in the mind of the person. It is a potential until it is declared as a fact. The second step is to begin assembling and practicing lore that has a basis in religious and magical Witchcraft. Since there is a huge volume of information online—not to mention printed or virtual books—the websites of various organizations, and many other sources, this next step is an obvious one. As a person accumulates various sources of information, they will undoubtedly start building a Witchy identity, and I have found that to be one of the first things that happens after someone declares that they are a Witch.

When a person has collected lore, adopted a new persona, and begun to have magical and religious experiences while experimenting, then at some point, they will have crossed a threshold and be ready for a truly serious start to their adopted faith and practices. So, they started with a declaration, built an identity, and began practicing their faith through experimentation. The next step is a form of dedication to the Witchcraft Deities that this person has identified as relevant, and such a working will truly begin their process of spiritual and magical development. They can, at this point, receive a traditional initiation or omit it altogether. The key is that if they persist and continue to evolve their workings, then they will move forward, and over time, establish for themselves a baseline tradition. It is even conceivable and quite likely that such a person will inadvertently trigger their own inner process and experience a powerful internal transformation, and this would be considered a kind of self-initiation.

This is how someone who has not been initiated into a tradition develops what could be considered their own tradition with an authentic psychic transformation functioning as their bonified initiatory status. I have known many individuals who would be classified as initiated Witches without ever having joined a coven and received a traditional initiation. These days, to underestimate someone who has achieved their own initiated tradition internally is to ignore a much larger percentage of practicing Witches than at any time previously. It is now a much stranger world for senior initiates; the comfortable boundary between the initiated and uninitiated has become blurred, and now it is quite irrelevant. When I remember the tragedy of my own coven experiences and how I might have evolved without having to undergo them and unlearn things that I had mistakenly adopted, I can easily sympathize with someone who chooses not to join a group.

What this does is make it a foolish notion to dismiss someone if they haven't been accepted into a proper coven and have undergone a traditional initiation. Excluding folks like this from a gathering or an open working in the community is a tragic mistake and one that I have continued to see happening in our various communities.

This is also why I always consider the history and past experiences of someone seeking teachings or initiation from my hand as an important assessment. Dismissing someone's past experiences and applying training and initiation in a cookie-cutter approach is the worst way to proceed in today's world. I have found that those who have persevered in their studies, practices, and experimentation will ultimately get to the same place and position that I have achieved. The only thing missing from the path of a solitary Witch is the all-important peer review and sanity check for practices and workings that I feel must accompany any kind of balanced growth. It is the community at large, whether as individual friends, accomplices, individuals, and groups, whether in personal encounters or through online media who can keep us objective and balanced, although I prefer personal exchanges and face-to-face meetings.

If we examine the path of the solitary Witch and the traditional coven-based Witch, there are some important stages where these paths converge, and there are rituals and actions that can help objectively define and maximize these steps into a fully vitalized practice of Witchcraft. If they are omitted in either path, then the outcome will be less clear and the ability to trigger internal psychic changes and growth will likely be suppressed or distorted over time. These stages are what I refer to as the essential types or stages for a Witch to become a fully capable practitioner of both magic and religious liturgy.

Here are the stages that I believe are critical to the fully empowered and self-realized Witch, and these stages are relevant, whether one has trod the path of traditional Witch or solitary Witch since even the training that one would receive in a coven could fall short of what is really needed.

1. Declaration and building an identity—becoming a Witch in fact.
2. Dedication to the Deities of Witchcraft.
3. Building a practice and performing magical and liturgical workings.
4. Initiation and psychic transformation.
5. Community work and social recognition.
6. Eldership, mentorship, and knowledge transfer.

What is important when assessing someone who has not received a traditional coven-based training regimen, nor a traditional initiation, is to use these six items as a checklist to determine where they are in the stages of development. Even if someone has received coven-based training and initiation, it would be prudent to check their accomplishments against these six stages since a lack in any of them would represent an incomplete process of growth.

A quick example of the lack of one or more of the six stages that can be used to measure one's growth can even be applied to me. The coven that I belonged to prohibited me from engaging and connecting with the Witchcraft and Pagan community. While I may have achieved my degrees and all the training that went with it, it was only after I left that coven that I began to connect with other Witches and Pagans in my greater community. Attending my first Pagan festival in 1980 was a shocking event for me because so much of what I had been taught was based on the sometimes-erroneous beliefs and practices of my teachers. It was only through exposure to other people and paths that my growth became balanced. As you can see, these stages are relevant to everyone, whether traditional or solitary.

We should examine these six stages and include any kind of rituals that might be pertinent to help them become objectified and impactful to the practicing Witch.

Declaration and Building an Identity

While there are no actual rituals for this stage, it is important that a person on the path of Witchcraft declare themselves as Witches. You don't have to make this announcement to the world, and digital media can even make this a somewhat safe thing to do if you have a flair for the dramatic. Still, someone besides you should know your intentions. Once that is done then you can build for yourself a proper public identity, dressing and acting in a way that gives you the kind of representation of your faith that meets your needs. This activity is optional since not everyone has the ability or the desire to represent themselves to the community at large. You don't have to go all-out, dressed in the goth fashion, but you should look and act like a Witch in suitable situations.

When I first started, many media Witches (like Sybil Leek, Witch Hazel, Alex Sanders, and Robert Cochrane) had a public persona and a private one, even assuming a magical name for both arenas. With the advent of the internet, you can declare that you are a Witch, build your identity, and commune with other like-minded individuals without assuming too great a risk to yourself. That was not the case when I was starting out back in the 1970s.

I have often found that traditional Witches lack a public persona and have not given much thought to building an identity as a Witch. They are in a coven, and they have been initiated. They are practicing their faith, but they have little or any kind of identification with being a Witch that they can use in a community setting. They have depth, but they do not have an outer identity that would characterize them as a Witch. Sometimes the leaders of the group are the public face, and the other members reside comfortably in the background.

Having a public persona could be considered more trouble than it's worth, but on the other hand, I believe that it is important for all Witches to have their own connections with the Witchcraft and Pagan community—at the very least to ensure that they are not isolated and dominated by the leaders of the group. Good coven leadership should encourage its members to communicate with other Witches and Pagans outside the group so they can know what is happening and understand the direction that the community is moving toward.

Those who have opted for a solitary path typically don't need to be encouraged to adopt a media persona and interact with their Craft friends and acquaintances, although some solitaries prefer to be secret and private in their work. I think that everyone who is practicing does need a peer group to guide and give assistance when it is needed. Some of the media Witches that I have encountered today who are self-taught and self-initiated seem to be deficient regarding the actual practices and the important transformational process of initiation, and so they lack depth. Then there are others who are balanced in their approach and who have accomplished a great deal completely on their own initiative.

Whatever you decide to do regarding your public persona or letting people in your community know that you are indeed a Witch, it is an important part of your development, whether you are learning the art of magic and the rituals of the Craft or if you are an elder with decades of experience. Witches may be called the Hidden Children of the Goddess, but we should not exist in isolation, whether we are solitary or in a coven.

Dedication to the Deities of Witchcraft

When I was initiated as a Witch decades ago, one of the things that I had to do was make an oath of secrecy regarding the coven and its teachings but also to swear fealty to the Goddess and God of the covenstead. It was part of my obligation as a religious adherent to the Craft and my coven that I gave this oath, and of course, I was informed about the penalty if I were to break it—that my magic would turn against me. While this oath is like the oath taken by the Candidate for the Masonic degree Entered Apprentice, it was echoed in all the following degrees through the York or Scottish rites. The same is also true of the Golden Dawn and the O.T.O. and other social and magical organizations—they all swore an oath and declared the penalty of their obligation.

However, I have found that the dedication to the Deities is not only an important initiation activity, but it functions as an important basis for my faith and practice as a Witch. Therefore, I believe that it is something that needs to be periodically renewed and reinforced as a powerful affirmation of the practice of a Witch. Therefore, I find myself periodically renewing my dedication to the Deities, giving them offerings, and showing gratitude for what I have received over the years.

A solitary Witch typically is not given an oath of fealty to swear to the Gods with the supposed obligations and penalties if that oath is broken. Yet this is something that must occur at some point in their studies and practices. This dedication is like getting confirmation in a Christian church, symbolizing that the adherent is now a fully functioning member of the organization of the church. There are important spiritual and magical reasons for making a dedication to one's chosen Witchcraft Deities, and this act is far more important than declaring yourself a Witch and building a persona. In fact, this action is the primary rite of functioning as a Witch, in my opinion, and it should neither be omitted nor should be done just once. If, for some reason, a seasoned solitary Witch has omitted this rite, then there is always time and an opportunity to fill in that void.

Some might ask why making an oath of fealty and dedication to the Witchcraft Goddess and God (and any other Deities that might be part of one's spiritual collective) is important. It has to do with spiritual accountability. In whose name do you act as a Witch, and to whom do you answer for the wrongs or infractions that you might have committed or those that have been committed against you? Who do you ultimately turn to for consolation, empowerment, and ultimately, a peaceful transition when you are at death's doorway? The answer, of course, is the specific named Deities of the Craft to whom you have aligned yourself in your practice. Without that proper alignment, there is no actual spiritual dimension to your work, and from a religious perspective, you are not a Witch unless you give honor and worship to the Deities of Witchcraft.

I unwittingly discovered this fact when I was a feckless youth who claimed to be a Witch, but who didn't own fealty to anyone or any Deity except myself. I could clearly sense the spiritual world all around me but acted coy or shy about committing to something far greater than myself. My ego was far too large for my actual accomplishments. That period was all too brief as I met the personal aspect of my Goddess who came to me in anger and sought to teach me a critical lesson about making empty claims and then fooling around with the Witchcraft rites and magical practices. She burned me, although briefly and with love, then helped me to obtain my faith. This happened several years before I was ever initiated into a coven. Ever since then, I have acknowledged my personal Goddess and sworn fealty and service to her at certain strategic times in my life.

In traditional covens, particularly some Gardnerian teaching covens, there is a boundary established between the Initiates in the regularly functioning coven and those who are seeking initiation and willing to go through a basic training period lasting a year and a day. This group is referred to as an outer court and requires that the trainee make a proper and full dedication at the start of their training. These student members of the outer court wear a white robe and the Initiates of the regular coven wear a black robe, at least when they are in the outer court. Gardnerians require their members to adhere to a regimen of ritual nudity, so they would only wear a black robe when not in a regular coven gathering. Sabbats would be ritual events when Dedicants, as they are called, would assemble with the Initiates, and the contrast of white and black robes would be a reminder of the differences between them.

While I approve of the action of performing a dedication rite to receive instruction, I feel that having an outer court where the students wear white robes with the Initiates wearing black to distinguish them is troubling. If a person is considered a worthy candidate, then why not just initiate them? Why keep a pretense of division between the white robes and the black robes? If there is a large influx of new Candidates into a coven and it would crowd out the current group, then just create a new coven with leaders selected from the current coven (but not the current HPs or HP).

The reason that some believe that there must be an outer court is the requirement for a trial period where the Dedicant can prove that they are worthy of initiation since there is a fear of bringing someone into the coven who might prove later to be unworthy. I think that such a logical argument is specious and unfounded. The first degree, in my opinion, is a trial degree. If a member fails to meet expectations, then they can be asked to leave or go on a sabbatical to determine what they truly wish to do. And, more importantly, it is okay if someone fails to realize their membership in the coven and drops out. It is part of the process of a seeker to be able to change their mind about their spiritual or magical path. Making divisions in a group will only create unwanted tensions and can lead to unequal treatment.

What is important is the dedication rite itself, and since that is what I believe should be an act that every Witch makes more than once, we should present it here for you to consider. I would recommend that everyone who considers themselves to be a Witch should examine this rite and develop their own version of it.

Dedication Rite

This rite should be performed in a consecrated and empowered circle, but it can be performed in any place that is private, such as in a grove or a backyard. The Dedicant should bring votive offerings to the Deities (one or more for each), and these can be food, drink, incense, oil, or a special gift (crystal or semi-precious stone). The best place to perform this rite is in front of a shrine with statues or markers for the Deities in plain sight. A dedication oath can be written before the rite occurs and then read at the proper moment. I am including an example of what might be used as a dedication oath. This dedication is performed to each of the Deities that are a part of your pantheon.

1. Bow before the focus point where the Deities are perceived to reside, then briefly kneel.
2. Light incense and candles, present the Deity with the offerings, and say:

   "O [Deity Name], I make an offering before you so that you may find it good and true. But I shall make a greater offering, and that is myself."

   Then bow down before the altar.
3. Say dedication:

   "I [Witch Name], in the presence of [Deity Name] do swear to serve, love, and worship you, making these offerings to you, but offering my life and spirit to be in your hands for whatever destiny you deem is suitable. May I receive your knowledge of hidden things and may I stand in the light of your power. I make this vow and dedicate myself to you and may my magic turn against me and the curse of the Gods be upon me if I break this most solemn and holy oath."

4. Offer the special gift, saying:

   "I give this precious offering to you; may it serve as a symbol of my love and faith."

5. If required, the Dedicant can also make an offering of their own blood, using a sharp knife to make a small shallow wound and to capture a drop or two onto a piece of cloth or parchment.[15] Then offer the blood to Deity with the rest of the offerings.

6. Stand up from the kneeling position, bow the head, and then extend the arms forward to the focus point, saying:

"From my head to my feet, and all that is between them, belongs to you forever."

BUILDING A PRACTICE AND SELF-INITIATION

Whether a Witch is an Initiate in a coven and a tradition or a solitary practicing adherent with a loose affiliation, building a practice and developing a discipline is a critical part of one's personal development. This development must be balanced between liturgical practices, such as the esbats and sabbats, and the practice of magic. I don't believe that a person can be balanced in their development unless they have learned how to perform either ritual magic or some collection of spells or folk magic and consider themselves a Witch. This may be my own bias, but I believe that a large part of Witchcraft is performing magical workings—it is the Craft part of Witchcraft. Since this is not a book for beginners, what we need to do is define what a balanced practice of liturgy and magic would look like. The reason such an assessment is important is that without some type of engagement of both magic and a direct engagement with the Gods, the internal process of transformative initiation will not be activated. The whole basis of this work is to describe the elements needed to ensure that the psychic dynamics of initiatory transformation can be active to either enhance a scripted initiation rite or to trigger one when it is needed.

---

15 During this procedure or any others herein, please use the utmost caution and care whenever skin is broken. Follow basic first aid practices of cleaning and dressing wounds, use sterile materials, and always dispose of blood and other bodily fluids responsibly. If bleeding ever becomes uncontrollable, promptly seek medical advice.

Performing material-based spell work without a divine agency or merely attending esbats and sabbats and other group or solitary workings will not activate one's internal psyche nor cause any triggering to occur. Even if someone were to participate in these kinds of activities for a lifetime, their inner psyche would likely be unaffected by these events. Where that can change is when an individual crosses liturgical practices with magical workings to produce a theurgical effect. It is the powers inherent in the divine that profoundly stimulate the inner psyche of a practitioner. Here is a list of the kinds of workings that will have an immediate effect on the inner mind and the soul of the Witch.

1. Godhead assumption—there is no surer way to profoundly stimulate the inner psyche than to practice this kind of exercise.

2. Sacramental communion—receiving food and drink that is consecrated can certainly alter one's mind, especially if it is done regularly and particularly to the person performing that exercise.

3. Performing ritual magic when under the influence of a partial godhead assumption.

4. Giving votive offerings to the Deities, especially if it is done regularly.

5. Meditation and prayer to the Deities.

6. Undergoing any kind of magical or religious ordeal or challenge that is not a scripted initiation rite.

I would recommend making these practices a regular part of your Witchcraft regimen if they are not already being utilized. Including all six of these practices will ensure that the internal psychic process of transformation will be activated and fully functioning in your Witchcraft workings. If these practices are completely omitted from your work, then you will not be able to constructively manage your own internal transformative process. In fact, I suspect that such a practice, devoid of contact with the Gods, would be quite static and even very boring.

This is the kind of dynamic practice of magic and liturgy that I would recommend. It will activate and empower an internalized transformative process and ensure that magical and religious practices have an optimal outcome. However, what I am proposing here is that a Witch need not wait for the allotment of scripted initiations to be bestowed upon them, if that is their option, nor to unwittingly stumble across a powerful and profound internal transformation if they do not belong to a traditional coven. Even if a person belongs to a tradition that considers only one initiation rite valid to be considered a member, the internal psychic transformation process, once activated, will bring them into stages and phases of their own subjective and personal initiation that cannot be accorded a predetermined script or a group acknowledgment.

It is my opinion that someone who has integrated the above practices into their Witchcraft praxis will experience strategic changes and cycles that will represent their own initiatory process. That process can be triggered using a self-initiation magical ritual, but the outcome and the process itself cannot be known until it occurs since it is so dependent on the individual and their own inner process.

What this strange fact about the internal initiatory process and the power of psychic transformation informs us about is that self-initiation represents a greater factor in the development of a Witch than what might have been previously considered. In some ways, it may even seem to negate the need for a traditional scripted initiation, although receiving such an external initiation into a defined tradition has its place in the development of a Witch. What I am not advocating is to devalue or deprecate traditional scripted initiations and replace them with a cyclic process of self-initiation. However, once that internal process is activated when intimately engaging with the Deities, then it is as if one has stepped outside of a tradition altogether and has assumed the path of the solitary Witch.

We have already examined the basic ritual patterns for the proposed fourth and fifth-degree initiations, and this pattern can be used to build a self-initiation rite that passes through all four elements and spirits. This initiation rite is a magical working much more so than a traditional scripted initiation since it doesn't truly confer any rights or obligations within that tradition. What it does confer is a time and a place where the internal psyche and one's external conscious reality merge for a brief period, producing a profound and visionary experience. In some ways, I find that kind of outcome to be more relevant in a subjective way than the results of a scripted initiation. The self-initiation might be self-directed and self-imposed, but it does require one or more witnesses to help objectify the initiatory experience.

I will present the ritual pattern for magical self-initiation, as it might be performed for the four elements in the next chapter (Part One, Chapter Five), along with some guidelines, material requirements, and preparations. I think that developing your own version of this ritual will help you master your own process of psychic transformation and lead you to ever greater levels of magical and spiritual achievement.

Community Work and Mentorship

Engaging in Witchcraft practices and working magic without engaging with one's community is a troubling omission and a deficit in the development of a practice. It doesn't matter if you belong to a coven and are actively engaged with that group if you are also neglecting the community at large. In every locality, the Witchcraft and Pagan community needs your support and engagement, and you need to be exposed to other traditions and perspectives to help keep yourself balanced and objective. Get to know the different groups and members of your community. Volunteer to help make community events and gatherings successful and represent your own tradition and path in a positive and constructive manner to others in your area. Certainly, if you are seeking to enlarge your group with quality members, then what could be a better source than the other people in your area who are practicing similar creeds?

Although many would not consider it appropriate to use your community connections to steal members of other groups to join your own, people do vote with their feet in expressing confidence (or the lack thereof) toward their existing group's leadership. I also think that it is a very bad form to exploit your community socially, fiscally, or sexually, but I am hoping that such an admonition would not be unnecessary.

One of the events that I have coordinated—or assisted in the communities that I belonged to—was to start a local Pagan festival with an organization that put it on every year. I have attended

Pagan festivals and conventions, performed many lectures and book signings, put together ritual workings for large groups, helped form a cross-tradition magical order, and many other activities. It is only since the advent of COVID-19 and moving to a new location that I have shunted my normal activities. I fully intend to become actively involved again in my community, as being sequestered and isolated goes against my principles requiring me to be a presence in my local community.

These are some of the many activities that you could assist or even inaugurate to benefit those other groups and individuals who are operating in your community. Some traditions urge their members to become politically engaged and to help foster change in the greater community. I am not against this approach since, as Witches and Pagans representing a small minority, we must be ever vigilant to protect our rights to worship in the manner of our choosing without outside interference or persecution.

Helping to maintain democratic institutions is a wise investment because when the freedom of some people is subverted, then the freedom of all is in question. Additionally, there are political battles happening right now that impact us as a nation and as a part of planet Earth. Ecology and conservation have long been a public concern, not to mention maintaining a secular society, the freedom of speech, the freedom to love whomever, and the freedom to privacy that protects all medical decisions, most particularly abortion. These causes are very important to Witches and Pagans, and so to those who feel so called, organizing and protesting are a visible method of seeking to make changes in our society.

Therefore, being engaged with our local communities, interacting with people, sharing information, and supporting political change are truly exemplary activities. Of course, since I am part of the older generation, I prefer such activities to be with real encounters with people and places. Yet, one could also do the same thing through the Internet and have just as much of an impact, but I truly feel that interacting with people in social settings is important because the Internet allows us to be less authentic and insulated from the consequences of our actions. That is just my opinion, and perhaps the best approach is to have a presence in both worlds.

Getting feedback from your peers is an important way to objectify your ideas and opinions, and to mitigate bad decisions and practices. It is also a way to build and achieve a reputation, and over time, even receive recognition and praise for activities that have benefited the greater community. These accolades should be unsought, of course, since doing something good for the community should be something that one would choose to do regardless of potential rewards. There is nothing more odious than someone who does something only because of the public attention or acclaim they might receive.

Ultimately, as you mature in your work and practice, it might be a good idea to gather like-minded individuals, or at least one individual, to pass your knowledge on to so that the legacy of your work is neither lost nor forgotten. In my long history of engaging with the community, particularly over the last decade or so, I have seen prominent members of our Witchcraft or Pagan communities pass away without having passed on their knowledge to a younger generation. When such an event occurs, the loss to the community is tragic and makes the overall collection of lore for us to consider or develop somehow diminished. That is why I believe that senior members of our community should receive recognition for their achievements and acquire at least one individual to mentor. There are rules for acting as a mentor, and there are rules for receiving lore from an elder.

A mentor relationship is a one-on-one interaction between an elder teacher and a student who seeks to acquire a full understanding of the knowledge that the elder possesses. I believe that this relationship should be equitable, respectful, and compassionate. It should also be temporary since at some point, the student will need to independently demonstrate their accumulated lore to make it their own. That means that the teacher doesn't own the student and should not try to continue to intercede or interrupt the student's process of making that lore their own. Conversely, the student should not try to pass themselves off as the originator of the knowledge that they acquired through mentorship. A student should give recognition to the teacher as the source of this lore, and the teacher should allow the student to deploy that knowledge through their own self-determination. If both parties are respectful and mindful of the other, then I believe that the transfer of knowledge will be successful.

I have chosen a slightly different path to pass on my knowledge to the younger generation as well as to my peers, and that is by writing books. There is a lot of written material about Witchcraft, but I have managed to encapsulate my peculiar techniques and methodologies of performing Witchcraft magic to the greater community by writing five books that attempt to fill the gaps of what is currently available in print or through the internet. It is my hope that others, perhaps even the younger generation, will take this knowledge and develop it beyond what I have managed to achieve over the decades and produce something even more unique and useful than what I have written in these five books.

This brings me to discuss the stage of life of a Witch or Pagan when they become old and are in their autumn years. Since I have entered that phase of life, this stage is much more of a concern to me than when I was a brash young man in my twenties. Like a confirmation within a coven, or recognition from a community, a Witch may celebrate passing this important milestone by a rite known as *Croning* for a woman, or *Senex* for a man. This is like getting a lifetime achievement and recognition award from the members of a group or community, but it also functions as a statement that a person has passed into a state of semi-retirement. That semi-state of retirement signifies that a person is no longer functioning as an active leader within the community or group, but that they can be consulted and sought out for arbitration or to give their opinions on matters of lore and practice.

A Croning or Senex rite is an event used to review the life of the celebrated elder, give them due recognition for their work, possibly transfer leadership responsibilities to others, and give some consecrated token or award to that elder as a sign of their passing to this stage. I have seen this token or reward vary, but it is typically some kind of plaque or commemorative document and a consecrated staff or walking stick. We begin life crawling on four legs, then graduate to two legs, and in old age, we come to having three legs, our two legs, and a walking stick. The consecrated staff could be seen as a token of seniority or authority, but the importance of this rite is that it honors the achievements of an elder.

A final rite of passage is the rite of the dead when a senior member has passed from this world to the next. Our discussion at the beginning of this work discussed the similarity of initiation and death, but the requiem rite is for the living who are left behind. The deceased is no longer living in this world, so their initiatory transformation has ended with the final event of their death. Probably the only ritual that I have ever seen that helps a person through the difficult and painful transition from life to death is found in the Tibetan Book of the Dead. I suspect that this tradition of life-to-death transition can also be found in other Buddhist rites for dying because only Buddhism seems to understand how to allay the trauma of undergoing dying, but I digress. Perhaps someday, someone will create a similar kind of ritual to aid a Witch who passes from life to death.

CHAPTER FIVE

SELF-INITIATION AND MAGICAL INITIATION OF THE FOUR ELEMENTS RITE

*"We take spiritual initiation when we become
conscious of the Divine within us, and thereby
contact the Divine without us."*

DION FORTUNE

Self-initiation has become a popular and singular practice in Witchcraft today. It is defined by both virtues and failings, so it can be a difficult path to travel. The virtues of taking this kind of pathway are that the Initiate is free of unwanted obligations, politics, and personal baggage often associated with the coven or group that might grant them a traditional initiation. The failings are that self-initiation is unable to be fully objectified and that the Candidate is not truly challenged as they would be if the initiation were conducted by others. What takes the place of a senior guide, teacher, or coven is an implacable faith and dedication to a specific Deity. The awakening of that Deity within one is the central Mystery to this work.

One of the most important factors in an initiation is that the Candidate should experience a kind of surrender and vulnerability that represents the beginning stages of a psychic transformation. This can be accomplished if the Candidate gives themself wholly and sincerely to their chosen Deity without any doubts, fear, or half-hearted commitments. This is a complete and total commitment to a specific Goddess or God that will act as the personal initiator and teacher of the Candidate. Therefore, the activated Mystery of this initiation is an empowered godhead assumption, blessing, and communion with one or more witnesses presiding. A witness or witnesses should attend this initiation ceremony to aid in its objectification, but the Candidate will perform this ritual to achieve an empowered initiation rite by their own hand.

The self-initiation ritual is a specifically magical rite that can be used to trigger an internal psychic transformation, simply because it uses a prepared godhead assumption rite as its central Mystery. I would assume that a Candidate performing this ritual has already performed a dedication rite and has undergone a period of devotion and godhead assumption practice before attempting to perform this rite. While this self-initiation rite represents a workable path for the solitary Witch, it should not be understood as a complete replacement for a traditional initiation since such a rite has its place and importance in the spiritual and magical path of the Initiate as well. What I am proposing with this ritual is an alternative that will in fact trigger a transformative initiation process.

So many years ago, I took this path myself because covens were very scarce and typically very picky about initiating someone. I performed simplified rites of self-initiation and had a very strong connection and dedication to my personal Goddess, and that went on for four years before I finally found a coven to petition for a traditional initiation. So, I had an experience with self-initiation myself well before it became a popular option. However, at that time, I didn't have the knowledge and expertise that I had developed over the decades to produce a ritual that would be a useful and potent alternative to a traditional initiation. I can provide such a rite to my readers in this work, making such an option a truly inspiring and empowering one.

Passage Through the Four Elements

We have already covered that an initiation can be considered as passing through the four elements and beyond into Spirit for the fifth degree. The passage through the four degrees represents the level of maturity that a self-initiated Witch would be able to authenticate to other Witches. Each element should represent the completion of a specific level of tasks and the Initiate should demonstrate this ability to others, preferably peers who are part of the Initiate's community and social world. I do believe that it is important to have friends and colleagues while traversing the path of a solitary Witch since these individuals will help to objectify what that Witch is experiencing and what they have accomplished through study and experimentation.

While we have covered ordeal and magical-based initiations for the traditional Witchcraft path for a fourth and fifth degree, using the foundation elements of Water and Spirit, I should mention that this initiation of the four elements, while similar, is quite different than those initiation patterns. The initiation of the four elements is a magical initiation ordeal set to the four elements for someone who either has decided to forgo traditional initiations altogether or seeks to augment their traditional initiation with those that are specifically magical ordeals. We should see these four elements as a continuous process of passing through the stages of personal spiritual and magical development.

I would also compare these four elements to the stages of the four seasons in the year, the four stages in the life cycle of a human being, and the four stages of the cosmogonic cycle. Associated with these four element seasons of initiation are a Goddess and God pair chosen from the Initiate's favorite pantheon. These pairs would represent birth or childhood, youth, lovers and parents, and elders for the elements of Earth, Air, Fire, and Water. The Deities would be aligned with the cosmogonic cycle of creation, age of ideation, age of death, and final dissolution. So, we would be looking at a Creator Pair, the Great King and Queen of a golden age, the Deities of life and death, and the Deity Pair of old age or seniority.

Of course, these four types of initiation would only be applicable if the solitary Witch desired to periodically pass through the four elements as part of their claim for self-initiation. If only a single initiation is considered relevant, then choosing one of the four elements or choosing Earth would be just as valid as passing through all four. However, I think that it is valid for a solitary Witch to claim that they passed through the self-initiation process of the four elements and have been fully tested and objectified as the final product of that passage.

If someone came to me for training and initiation and made this claim, and they could prove it with their magical diary and witness affidavits, then I would happily confer on them the full legitimacy and recognition of being a spiritual and magical leader in my tradition of Witchcraft. I am not certain that other leaders or groups would be so generous, but I believe that we need to consider an individual's true status before adopting them into a tradition.

The way that I would characterize the four initiations and their preparation tasks is somewhat different than how I would characterize a four-degree system within a traditional Witchcraft initiation system. Since a solitary Witch would typically forgo training other Initiates and functioning as a coven or group leader, the approach would represent personal accomplishments within a solitary path. Here is how I would characterize the accomplishments that would have to be performed before the initiation Mystery rite for that element was performed.

1. FIRST DEGREE—Earth: A mastery of the rituals of the moon and sun, their associated celebrations and Mystery rites, and the skills associated with Earth, such as herbal magic, healing magic, material-based spells, divination (Tarot), and meditation. A primary level of a godhead dedication and preparations for a godhead assumption would also be required.

2. SECOND DEGREE—Air: A mastery of higher forms of magic, such as elemental magical workings and advanced energy magic, tool consecration (including triple consecration), grove workings, astrological divination, deep trance, crystal scrying, pendulum and dowsing works, spirit travel, and dream/symbols interpretation. A secondary level of godhead dedication and periodic godhead assumption is practiced through the lunar cycle (Lunar Mysteries).

3. THIRD DEGREE—Fire: A mastery of celestial magic, talismanic magic, deeper Mysteries of the moon and the sun, mastery of magical evocation and spirit conjuration, goetic and dark magic, mastery of the Qabalah, Neoplatonism or another spiritual philosophic system, outer court liturgical workings for the community at large, functioning as a personal religious cult leader and priest/ess, geomancy, runes, and other systems of divination (I-Ching), and expertise in astrology and astrological counseling. A tertiary level of a godhead dedication and regular godhead assumption is practiced through specific celestial observations (lunar mansions, decans, etc.).

4. FOURTH DEGREE—Water: A mastery of sacramental theurgy, developing and performing a magical mass and benediction rites, mastery of consecration, generating amulets and functioning as a liaison for a specific Deity to the community, full godhead personification, mastery of temple and grove workings, recognition as a community elder, adopting a rigorous discipline of godhead embodiment, acting as a godhead oracle, giving blessings, and aiding in community magical endeavors. A quaternary level of a godhead dedication and adopting the godhead personification ordeal for a period not less than five years.

As you can see, achieving all four levels prior to passing through the associated initiation of the element would be quite demanding and would likely take a lifetime of work and effort. Even having passed through the first two elements would represent a period not less than five years of work, and each level beyond that would take even more time to experience and master all that is required of each of the final two degrees. To tell someone that you have passed through the initiations of all four elements would be the same as saying that you are a master of the Witchcraft arts. I am certain that other disciplines could be added to these four elements, representing other arts and abilities, such as herbalism, material-based thaumaturgy (Hoodoo and folk magic), metal and woodcraft, and much more.

GODDESSES AND GODS
OF THE FOUR SEASONS

As stated previously, the initiation of the four elements requires the operator of this rite to select four pairs of Deities to act as the representatives of the four stages of the human life cycle and the cosmogonic cycle. These pairs of Deities can be selected from any pantheon. They should roughly fit the pattern of a Creator Pair, the Great King and Queen of a golden age, Deities of life and death, and the Deity Pair of old age or seniority. The associations don't have to be perfect or exact but would represent a creative interpretation of these godheads as they would relate to the mythic pattern used in this initiation. I would also recommend that when each of these initiations for the element is performed, the Initiate will revisit and possibly revise this ritual since, over time and with experience, the development of this ritual will be made more precise and exact regarding the internal spiritual process of the Initiate.

Here's how I would select the four pairs of Deities if I were performing a version of the rite using either the Welsh mythos, the Grail mythos, or the Egyptian mythos. This should help you to build up your own set of Deity correspondences for this ritual. I have divided the four elements into their respective polarities, where receptive is the archetypal feminine and creative is the archetypal masculine. To use a set of Deities, you will need to develop an image of them and a short, memorized invocation to each.

Element	Welsh Mythos	Grail Mythos	Egyptian Mythos
Earth Receptive	Modron	Condrie	Nuit
Earth Creative	Manawydan	Perceval	Ra
Air Receptive	Arrianrhod	Guinevere	Isis
Air Creative	Bran	Arthur	Osiris
Fire Receptive	Aerowen	Elain of Corbenic	Hathor
Fire Creative	Mabon	Lancelot	Horus
Water Receptive	Cerridwen	Nimue	Maat
Water Creative	Arawn	Merlin	Thoth

The rest of the attributes of the four elements are built into the ritual structure itself, so we don't need to discuss them here. What is left to discuss is the initiation ritual itself. This is the suggested ritual structure, and to use it, you will need to develop it so that it represents your self-initiation.

Ritual of the Self-Initiation of the Four Elements

The circle has been set up and consecrated and all preparations are complete. Witnesses are seated outside the circle for most of the rite until called into the center by the Candidate who is performing the ritual. The Candidate (called the Celebrant) is fully prepared to perform this rite for the given element and has met the requirements established for this stage. They are garbed in robes of their choosing, after having bathed, anointed themself, and performed a period of meditation.

The Celebrant stands in the center of the circle, armed with a consecrated dagger, bows to the western watchtower, and recites a short declaration of their identity, starting with their name, objective, accomplishments, and spiritual alignments. This declaration seeks to quickly answer the questions of who is seeking to perform this rite (Craft name), what they expect to accomplish, by what right they claim to have the experience to proceed with this working, and who is their sponsor Deity. This declaration should be brief and memorized.

Pyramid of Empowerment

1. Celebrant proceeds to the eastern watchtower and therein draws an invoking pentagram of the element of the initiation (Earth: receptive, Air: creative, Fire: creative, Water: receptive) to the base of the watchtower, then to the height, draws an invoking pentagram of Spirit creative (masculine) or receptive (feminine), depending on the polarity of the element. Celebrant draws a narrow invoking spiral to connect the two pentagrams, ending with the dagger pointing to the center point between them and exhaling the breath. Then the Celebrant invokes the God of Air and says the following line:

   "I call and summon thee, O [God Name] of the Powers of the Element of Air, to be a witness to this ordeal that I seek to achieve."

2. The Celebrant proceeds to the northern watchtower and therein performs the same actions as previously, generating

a pylon into the northern watchtower. Then the Celebrant invokes the God of Earth and says the following line:

"I call and summon thee, O [God Name] of the Powers of the Element of Earth, to be a witness to this ordeal that I seek to achieve."

3. The Celebrant proceeds to the western watchtower and therein performs the same actions as previously, generating a pylon into the western watchtower. Then the Celebrant invokes the God of Water and says the following line:

"I call and summon thee, O [God Name] of the Powers of the Element of Water, to be a witness to this ordeal that I seek to achieve."

4. The Celebrant proceeds to the southern watchtower and therein performs the same actions as previously, generating a pylon into the southern watchtower. Then the Celebrant invokes the God of Fire and says the following line:

"I call and summon thee, O [God Name] of the Powers of the Element of Fire, to be a witness to this ordeal that I seek to achieve."

5. The Celebrant proceeds to the east, turns, and travels to the center of the circle and therein performs the same actions as previously, generating a pylon into the center of the circle. Then the Celebrant invokes their personal godhead and says the following line:

"I call and summon thee, O [God/dess Name] of the Powers of my Inner Being, to be a witness to this ordeal that I seek to achieve."

6. The Celebrant returns to the altar, exchanges the dagger for a sword, then proceeds to the eastern watchtower and draws a line from the pylon placed therein to the center of the circle in the zenith, thus connecting them.

7. The Celebrant proceeds to the north, then the west, and then the south, and performs the same action as in the east.

8. The Celebrant proceeds to the east and draws a line with the sword from the eastern watchtower to the north, continuing to the west, south, and ending again in the east. The pylon pyramid is now set. The Celebrant returns to the altar and exchanges the sword for the wand.

9. The Celebrant proceeds to the east and walks a spiral widdershins circuit toward the center of the circle, passing the east three times. The pyramid vortex is now empowered.

Gate of the Mysteries

1. The Celebrant stands in the center of the circle, facing east, and proceeds to the east, turns, and faces the west. The Celebrant declares:

"I face the three challenges."

2. The Celebrant draws an invoking spiral to the southeast and envisions the guide, saying:

"My first challenge is to conquer fear."

3. The Celebrant draws an invoking spiral to the northeast and envisions the guardian, saying:

"My second challenge is to overcome arrogance."

4. The Celebrant draws an invoking spiral to the west, envisions the gateway of the west and the ordeal, saying:

"My third challenge is to thwart hubris."

5. The Celebrant draws an invoking spiral to the zenith in the center of the circle and envisions the fourth way or resolution of the ordeal, saying:

"The key to overcoming all challenges is the surrender to love."

6. The Celebrant stands before the west, and proceeds slowly, traveling from the east to the western watchtower, makes the sign of opening the veil of the Mysteries, and steps forward, turns, and feels the light cascading from above the western watchtower to the floor.

7. The Celebrant proceeds to the center of the circle and imagines walking down a stairway to the darkened underworld. In the center, the Celebrant turns to face the west. They stand and meditate for a short period.

Cycle of Light and Darkness, Life and Death

1. The Celebrant, still holding the wand, proceeds to the north, bows, and draws an invoking pentagram of Earth, saying:

    "Birth unfolds into youth, a time of growing and learning."

2. Then the Celebrant invokes the Goddess of Earth and says the following line:

    "I call and summon thee, O [Goddess Name] of the Powers of the Element of Earth, to be a witness to this ordeal that I seek to achieve."

3. The Celebrant proceeds across the circle to the south, bows, and draws an invoking pentagram of Fire, saying:

    "Youth becomes beauty and filled with desire, as the lustful lovers."

4. Then the Celebrant invokes the Goddess of Fire and says the following line:

    "I call and summon thee, O [Goddess Name] of the Powers of the Element of Fire, to be a witness to this ordeal that I seek to achieve."

5. The Celebrant proceeds widdershins to the east, bows, and draws an invoking pentagram of Air, saying:

    "Desire is manifested as children, and life passes into parenthood."

6. Then the Celebrant invokes the Goddess of Air and says the following line:

    "I call and summon thee, O [Goddess Name] of the Powers of the Element of Air, to be a witness to this ordeal that I seek to achieve."

7. The Celebrant proceeds across the circle to the west, bows, and draws an invoking pentagram of Water, saying:

    "Desire becomes cold, life brittle, but the heart is full of wisdom. So it shall be until death."

8. Then the Celebrant invokes the Goddess of Water and says the following line:

    "I call and summon thee, O [Goddess Name] of the Powers of the Element of Water, to be a witness to this ordeal that I seek to achieve."

9. The Celebrant proceeds to the center of the circle, facing the east. Draws in the nadir an invoking pentagram of spirit creative (masculine), saying:

    "From birth to death, the continuous cycle of light and darkness, guided from each state by the hand of the Great Mother, who symbolizes the ever-changing spirit of mortal existence."

10. Then the Celebrant invokes their personal godhead and says the following line:

    "I call and summon thee, O [God/dess Name] of the Powers of my Inner Being, to manifest within me so that you and I are one and the same."

11. The Celebrant proceeds to the center of the circle where a small altar is placed with a head wreath, circlet, or diadem and a small bottle of consecrated oil. There is also an appropriate chalice for drinking and a dish of bread or cakes. The Celebrant self-anoints their forehead with oil, dons their head wreath or circlet, and then stands slightly away from the altar. The Celebrant then performs the full godhead assumption.

12. Once this action is completed, they invite the Witnesses to come to the center of the circle, and they bow before the Celebrant to perform an impromptu adoration, saying praises to the Deity that the Celebrant has assumed.

13. The Celebrant proceeds to the altar and performs the rite of consecrating the wine and the bread or cakes. They then invite the Witnesses to come and kneel before them where the Celebrant gives each a drink from the chalice and one of the pieces of bread or cake. Then the Celebrant places their hands upon the Witnesses' heads and gives them a sacramental blessing.

14. Once the communion has ended, the Celebrant stands away from the center altar and gives silent thanks to the Deity that they have assumed and performs the parting, allowing themself to slowly return to normal. Then the Celebrant says:

"I have achieved the empowerment and blessing of the element of [Earth, Air, Fire, Water] and I stand before Witnesses to this act. Let it be known that I am an Initiate of [Earth, Air, Fire, Water]—So Mote it Be!"

Return to the Light

1. The Celebrant and Witnesses sit in meditation for a period in the center of the circle, absorbing all that has occurred within the chamber of the Mysteries.

2. Once this is complete, the Celebrant takes up the wand, the altar is taken away, the Witnesses stand to the side, and the Celebrant continues the rite, facing the west and making the sign of the closing of the veil. The gateway exhortations

represent the relationship of the solitary Witch to the general community at large, which they must honor and follow.

3. The Celebrant proceeds to the western watchtower, turns, and faces the east, saying:

"I face the three virtues of my Craft and vow to practice them."

4. The Celebrant draws an invoking spiral to the northwest and envisions the guide, saying:

"My first virtue is to be charitable to my fellow members of the Craft."

5. The Celebrant draws an invoking spiral to the southwest and envisions the guardian, saying:

"My second virtue is empathy, so I will seek to understand the point of view of my fellow members of the Craft."

6. The Celebrant draws an invoking spiral to the east and envisions the gateway of the east and the ordeal, saying:

"My third virtue is consensus, so I will seek to know the various opinions of my fellow members and discover a united direction for our clan."

7. The Celebrant draws an invoking spiral to the zenith in the center of the circle and envisions the fourth way or resolution of the ordeal, saying:

"May I learn to give these virtues from myself to all humankind, and thereby achieve wisdom."

8. The Celebrant stands before the east, and proceeds slowly, traveling from the west to the eastern watchtower, makes the sign of opening the second veil of the Mysteries, and steps forward, turns, and feels the light cascading from above the eastern watchtower to the floor.

9. The Celebrant proceeds to the center of the circle, imagining walking up a stairway to the brilliant sunrise. In the center, the Celebrant turns to face the east. Stand and meditate for a brief period. The ordeal is completed.
10. The Celebrant draws a sealing spiral each to the four watchtowers, the zenith, and nadir.

The ritual is ended.

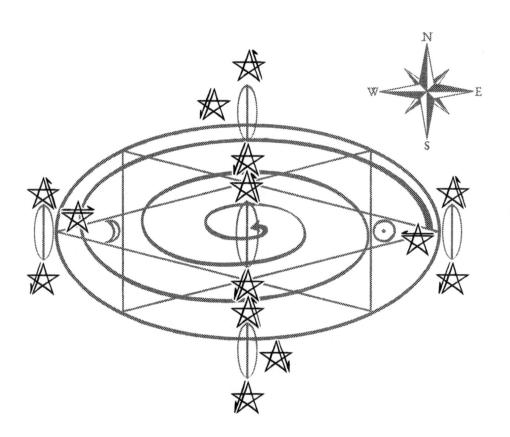

Diagram of the Self Initiation of the Four Elements Rite

PART TWO

TRANSFORMATIONAL INITIATION

CHAPTER ONE

WHAT IS TRANSFORMATIVE INITIATION—A DEFINITION

"Knowing reality means constructing systems
of transformations that correspond, more or less
adequately, to reality."

JEAN PIAGET

Change is an inescapable reality that confronts us every day of our lives. There are times when we embrace change and undergo it willingly, and there are times when we deny and resist change, and then it happens anyway. However, there is a kind of change that is powerful and internal to our mental processes. It is that kind of change that I am referring to when I talk about psychic transformations. Sometimes external events will trigger these changes, but often, they occur with little or no external stimulus or warning. The basis for this kind of change is not difficult to perceive from an external perspective, but it is typically quite difficult to either know or predict that these changes are going to occur when it is one's own internal and external reality.

What occurs when an internal transformation is about to happen is that one's identity and internal processes are no longer capable of coping with what is happening in one's life. Psychic identity is based on how you see yourself, including your beliefs, objectives, and the direction that you believe your life must follow to achieve your desires and avoid that which would block or derail that progress. Identity is then your definition of self, values, beliefs, motivations, and ambitions.

When any of these components fail to achieve the cohesive results that you are pursuing, then the resulting disharmony begins to oblate your beliefs and your concept of self. A series of these occurrences happening consecutively will cause the definition of the self to shift or become unstable. If change is undesirable and resisted, then it will ultimately cause the self to collapse, manifesting as a kind of internal death of the ego.

Everyone comes to a point in their life when their ideals, beliefs, and identity become outmoded and they can no longer successfully achieve their objectives or meet their expectations. Often, all that is needed is to adjust and make minor changes, discard obsolete ideals, or seek a new and reformed life perspective. However, someone who is walking a spiritual and magical path will discover that their beliefs and identity are so incapable of dealing with what they are experiencing that they will need to completely change who they are to accurately process these experiences.

Spiritual teachings inform us that the best way to undergo this kind of change is to surrender instead of resist. Many spiritual traditions teach this important point, and even the traditions of Witchcraft and Paganism discuss the importance of approaching the Deities with a humble heart and proceeding through the Mysteries with the passwords of perfect love and trust.

The word "trust" used here denotes the need for surrendering to the will of the Gods when the time comes for psychic and internal change. This is the reason for being blindfolded and bound when entering the sacred boundaries of the magic circle to receive an elevation through a traditional coven initiation. This is a surrender, and a willingness to sacrifice one's old life with love and trust so that what replaces it will be greater than what was lost.

Internal psychic change, then, for someone on a mystical and magical path, would be precipitated through exposure to the Deities and entities of the paranormal world of Spirit. Engaging with the Deities and spirits while working various types of magic will guarantee that a Witch will find themself periodically undergoing an internal psychic transformation. The reason for this is that all identities, beliefs, values, and ambitions are imperfect and flawed, to some degree. Encountering a Deity and experiencing it fully will not only show one's internal imperfections, contradictions, and erroneous beliefs, but it will trigger the internal archetypes of the self and foster a psychic trans-formation. A Deity is not perfect itself, but it acts like an archetypal dark mirror that reflects accurately who we really are and shows us our reflection, much to our fascination and horror.

Transformations are forms of internal psychic realizations that occur in a dramatic, dreamlike state of mind that produces disturbing dreams, visions, and synchronistic external occurrences that cause seekers to question the very foundation of their being. They force individuals to confront their actions, beliefs, and internal rules that are now seen as flawed, inadequate, and failing to provide the self with any kind of certainty or security. The resulting confusion and despair heralded the beginning of the cyclic process where the old identity and its beliefs and values die and are replaced with a new identity. Yet, in between the death of the ego and its restoration in a new form, the self undergoes fragmentation and disintegration, while visions and archetypal struggles help to define and determine a new self. It is a cyclic process of death and rebirth, darkness and light that individuals undergo, and that cyclic nature is a foundation for the process of all life.

Cycles of light and darkness that are a part of the transformation cycle are also to be found in the diurnal cycle and circadian rhythm of all living things. We are awake and conscious, and we sleep and dream while unconscious of the external world. When we undergo a transformative change, it is very much like the cycle of wakefulness and sleep that marks us as living beings. The cycle of psychic transformation emulates the cycle of wakefulness and sleep because that is the very process through which we are rested, restored, and re-energized. Psychic death and rebirth have a similar pattern to what we undergo when we sleep, dream, and surrender ourselves to the twilight consciousness of the unconscious state.

While the pattern of wakefulness and sleep is like the pattern of psychic death and rebirth, the process of this cycle is far more dramatic, compelling, and filled with the archetypes and symbols of transformation enacting the endless story of self-transformation. It is the story of the ordeal of the hero or heroine, and it resonates throughout the psyche of the individual and the collective consciousness of the culture.

This cycle often occurs in full wakefulness, but it is more like a series of dreams, visions, nightmares, and internal psychic struggles that may take many days or even years to resolve. This process interrupts and intrudes on our lives, forcing us to deal with it directly, regardless of whatever else is occurring. It has stages, and it is an overall progression from the psychic stage of night into day, where the old self is sacrificed in the dark night of the soul, and the new self is born from the reoccurring light. For this reason, a person may experience periods of peace and inactivity when one stage is completed and just before another begins. When someone has passed through an entire cycle and achieved psychic rebirth, then it can be correctly assumed that the peace and fulfillment that follows will not last forever. One transformative cycle is followed by another, and another, throughout life until death.

I call this endless series of cycles "the process" because it is the very spiral path that leads us to become better and more fulfilled human beings. The process is stimulated and assisted by the Deities, so one might consider calling it the fate of an individual seeker. However, it is not something that is predetermined or that negates our precious freedom of choice. The process only continues to act in our life when we choose to allow it, and it can become dormant if we turn from the Gods to engage in other things in life.

Still, if we choose to turn away from the process, then we are placing ourselves into a dangerous potential where our own internal psyche may erupt in a long-delayed and overdue change and we will have no control in mitigating its disastrous consequences. It should be noted that once the process is initiated, it is difficult or even impossible to turn away or ignore it for more material concerns. Those of us who have become aware of our internal process are seemingly subject to its whims and haunted by its demanding appearance in our lives. It is no surprise that being altogether ignorant of this godhead-inspired process of internal transformation is the only guarantee of internal peace and placid uneventfulness—at least one can hope for that to be the case.

Curiously, undergoing this cyclic process of internal transformation has within it the same pattern that victimizes those suffering from mental illnesses, particularly schizophrenia and depression, except those who suffer from these maladies might not resolve their crisis, and would instead experience the full and painful death of the self without any psychic rebirth or ascension. It is presumed by mental health experts that one out of eight of people suffer from mental illness, so the prevalence of this one-sided pattern is more likely and frequent than most people realize.[16]

There is a difference between those who undergo this process and experience an empowering psychic rebirth and those who completely lose their identity and never return to full conscious self-awareness. It is the difference between madness and apotheosis, the destruction of the self without rebirth or rebirth, and conscious ascension. Both transformative processes go through a similar pattern where the self is disintegrated, but the path of apotheosis and rebirth has a second part that leads from the darkness of the psychic underworld to the world of light and full consciousness. We would be wise to review these differences so we can understand that our actions and spiritual alignments can help us make the transition from darkness and psychic death to light and psychic rebirth when undergoing this ordeal.

MADNESS AND APOTHEOSIS

Madness and genius are often equated, although to compare malady and suffering to visionary insight is likely a form of sophistry. It also devalues the fact that everyone who passes through the transformative process, whether successful in their efforts for psychic rebirth or having failed in that task, experiences a certain amount of internal suffering and difficulty. Even those who have an incredibly positive experience undergoing a traditional scripted initiation will also, over time, experience hardship, suffering, doubt, and confusion. I count myself in that category because even though I experienced a kind of exalted ascension after my two initiations into traditional Witchcraft, on the other side of that process, the fallout I experienced after the coven fell apart left me with much guilt, regret, and internal pain. It ensured that I would never sell short the dark side of initiation and that lessons delayed are lessons learned later with greater pain and loss.

Much of the brain chemistry for mental illness is becoming clearer through the efforts of science. Genetics and environment play a decisive role, but so do trauma and tragedy. Outside occurrences can

---

16 "Mental Disorders." *World Health Organization (WHO)*, https://www.who.int/news-room/fact-sheets/detail/mental-disorders. Accessed 12 Oct. 2023.

act as a trigger for an internal brain structure and chemistry that is set for the potential of the occurrence of mental illness. However, transformation is the key to both those who have the potential for a psychic breakdown and those who are ready for a higher state of being.[17]

There are critical differences between these two states of potential, such as brain structure and chemistry, but also in the state or strength of the willpower of one and the total lack of willpower in the other. Both paths will incur a state of vulnerability to the subject, but one will possess an inherent internal strength, trust, and optimism, and the other an inherent weakness, distrust, belief in conspiracies, delusions, and an overall pessimistic outlook. While both are undergoing the death of the self, only one of them believes in the possibility of self-reformation and reconstitution.

As I have previously stated, the impact of mental illness on the self consists of its disintegration, but the whole process of reintegration and rebirth is not followed nor possible. The transformative cycle consists of only one-half of the overall process for those who will undergo the death of the self, but not the rebirth. While it is possible that a combination of brain chemistry correction (drug therapy) and functional group therapy will alleviate the suffering, only some form of radical transformative therapy can assist in rebuilding the fragmented self, ultimately assisting the patient in some level of recovery. This is what hallucinogenic drug therapy (LSD) was thought to do for certain kinds of mental illnesses, and in the present, these kinds of therapies are being explored once again.[18]

It is quite possible for persons undergoing transformative initiation to lose their way and find it difficult or impossible to experience a psychic rebirth, yet it is quite unlikely for this to happen if the seeker has developed certain spiritual alignments and possesses the inner strength and optimism necessary to revision themselves,

---

17 "Information about Mental Illness and the Brain—NIH Curriculum Supplement Series—NCBI Bookshelf." *National Center for Biotechnology Information*, https://www.ncbi.nlm.nih.gov/books/NBK20369/. Accessed 11 Oct. 2023.

18 "Psychedelic Medicine: A Re-Emerging Therapeutic Paradigm—PMC." *PubMed Central (PMC)*, https://www.ncbi.nlm.nih.gov/pmc/articles/PMC4592297/. Accessed 12 Oct. 2023.

precipitating a psychic rebirth. The rebirth is always the building and production of a new materialized identity, and the greatest task is to interpret what they have experienced and the knowledge that it has given them something intelligible to their family and peers.

Genius, as experienced in the full cycle of the death and rebirth of the identity, consists of the wisdom and insights that are gained by going through this cyclic process. These insights and intuitions are never lost nor diminished. Once the process of cyclic transformation starts in the mind and soul of the seeker, external occurrences, meetings with remarkable people, and a kind of life-based teleology manifest to guide them through the vicissitudes of life.

Once started, the process will lead seekers on the path that they should be following, giving inspiration, visions, and assistance as required. The process also helps to prepare the seeker for renewed transformations and helps to interpret what has been experienced when the cycle has been completed. While I have restrained myself from characterizing the process too much so that it might have a name and an identifiable being, I do believe that it could be seen in that manner. When the higher self as one's personal godhead evolves to a mature extent, then that being and its process meld together to become the brilliant godhead and inspired genius that goes along with the seemingly endless path of the seeker.

Another variation is to consider the path of the mystic, particularly the Christian mystic. Like the pattern of mental illness, Christian mystics seek to renounce the material world and their identity within it and remain in the habitat of their spiritual discipline for the duration of their lives. They experience the disintegration of the old self, but they do receive a new identity, yet it is wholly within the embrace of their God and their spiritual service. They enter the underworld of their soul and seek to make it like the house of God, where they remain in service for the rest of their days. Thus, there are similarities to the half cycle of those suffering from mental illness, but it is the strength of the seekers' faith that keeps them from experiencing the harm of not being able to rebuild themselves. They receive a new identity, but it is bound to their God and restrained by a strict regimen of practices. Without a fully formed material-based identity, a mystic can be subject to periods of darkness and despair, called the Dark Night of the Soul.

Depression and the
Dark Night of the Soul

It has become something of a fad over the last several years for Initiates, especially Golden Dawn Initiates, to talk about how they have undergone the experience of the Dark Night of the Soul. As we have defined it, the requirements for such an experience would require a complete renunciation of the material world and one's material-based identity. Existing in such a state of mind makes one vulnerable to doubt, desolation, despair, and feelings of rejection and isolation, all within an intense spiritual context. Still, there seems to be the consensus amongst this group that all magicians at some point retire from the world (and in a sense, renounce it) and undergo the mystical rigors of the Dark Night of the Soul while seeking union with the One.

Strangely, I seem to be one of the few who finds issues with this kind of explanation, and I have respectfully disagreed with those who have espoused this perspective. I think that it has more to do with a mystical approach to the godhead than a magical approach, and there are also the issues of chronic or situational depression, isolation, and despair that have really nothing to do with spiritual ascension. In clinical depression, removing oneself from the world is a common symptom, and strong feelings are often replaced with a feeling of numbness, stasis, or apathy.

The real question then is whether the iconic Dark Night of the Soul is real for mystics and magicians alike. Some have also questioned whether there is a difference between the two paths since they seem to lead to the same ultimate place. Since I have defined the mystical process of transformation as being half a transformation cycle, then there should be a real difference between magicians and mystics. I would include Witches and Pagans in the latter group because magic is integral to their approach to religious beliefs and practices.

As a Witch, I cultivate mystical experiences and encounters in the magical workings that I perform, and I mix them when practicing forms of sacramental theurgy. However, there is a vast difference between having mystical experiences within a magical context and functioning as a mystic. They are not at all the same thing, in my opinion, and I believe that some occultists seem to confuse these two very different processes. Magical practitioners can and do have mystical experiences, but they are not practicing mystics. This is because a Witch or Pagan practicing magic does so with a spiritual purpose that is quite different from that of a mystic. This differentiation leads me to make some theological considerations regarding the context through which the Dark Night of the Soul occurs, both from a monotheistic and a Pagan perspective.

From the perspective of Abrahamic religious traditions (and, to an extent, within Western metaphysical philosophy), humanity is in a fallen state and requires redemption to be spiritually fulfilled. The first step in finding redemption is to renounce the material world since it's the source of all that is fallen, separate, and distinct from the godhead. The physical world, and all it contains, is unredeemed. Thus, the seeker on the path of spiritual redemption first recognizes the fallen state of humanity and the abject condition of the material world and renounces it. Yet, once this is done, they will undergo and experience probably the most difficult and bitter isolation imaginable to begin the process of achieving redemption. Let's keep in mind that this is the mystical path to redemption (union with God) and not the general path to redemption (blessings and forgiveness of sins) open to all faithful adherents.

Yet to achieve redemption and salvation, mystics must transcend all that binds them to their physical lives, egocentric sentiments, and their material circumstance in life to truly realize the hidden presence of the godhead. Only by employing this extreme degree of self-sacrifice and world rejection is redemption possible, for without it, the seeker can't cross the boundary that separates humanity from God, which is the sole objective. (Of course, there are other ways that the layperson can receive a certain kind of redemption for their faith, such as being redeemed through the intercession of Jesus Christ, nevertheless, the path of the mystic is the most onerous and difficult to undertake.)

However, in my opinion, a modern Witch or Pagan has no need for any kind of redemption because they don't subscribe to the belief that there is a separation of spirit and matter, or that matter is in a fallen state along with humanity. We don't believe in original sin, so we don't need to be redeemed. In fact, the whole Lurian Qabalistic legacy doesn't make a lot of sense to someone who is a modern

Witch or Pagan since the idea that spirits are trapped as *sparks* in the dross material world has the same kind of antinomian quality associated with theologies that reject the divine nature of the natural world (such as sects of Gnosticism, Fundamentalist Christianity, and Neoplatonism). Since Pagans embrace all material life and consider it to be sacred and imbued with spirit, there is no need to somehow either elevate or reject matter.

To Witches and Pagans, spirit and matter are unified in emulation of the One, which is the nameless source of everything. Matter is imbued with consciousness, and everything is therefore connected. If one wishes to experience the divine, then nature is the principal place on which one should focus their attention. I have found this philosophy to be an important remedy for the disease of duality that appears to plague most Western religious and philosophical systems. Also, there is no division between Deity and humanity since the individual *God/dess Within* is also synonymous with the Cosmic Deity. If there is no fall and no original sin for Witches and Pagans, nor any kind of division between the godhead and humanity, then redemption is quite irrelevant and so is the Dark Night of the Soul. All that is required for one to learn to see and experience the world as a holistic fusion of spirit, mind, and matter, resolving itself into the One is to approach it and life itself without judgment.

The term "Dark Night of the Soul" was a phrase invented by the Spanish poet and Christian mystic St. John of the Cross and given to the title of a series of poems he wrote (*La Noche Oscura del Alma*), even though the process he describes was certainly not his invention. The poems he wrote depict the archetypal process or journey that he underwent when he sought a more perfect union with God. It is called the "Dark Night" because it symbolizes the ordeal that the soul encounters when in that intermediate state between renouncing the world and reaching the illuminating presence of the Deity. It is an experiential process that can and does happen for years, and in some documented cases, it is only intermittently resolved.

According to St. John of the Cross, this process has two stages; the first is a purification of the senses, and the second and more difficult, is the purification of the soul. The purpose of both ordeals is to eliminate all irrelevant and worldly things from the senses, mind, and soul of the seeker and thereby to become worthy of union with the Absolute. Purification of the senses is accomplished through a form of deprivation, where the mind and body are put in a situation where all sensory distractions are slowly attenuated until the life of the monk is one that is regulated by religious services, prayer, meditation, contemplation, work, and the basic needs of plain food and drink, rudimentary shelter, austere clothes, and little or no creature comforts whatsoever.

Purification of the soul is accomplished through strict forms of prayer, meditation, contemplation, and the enforcement of disciplines such as silence, isolation, self-humility, surrendering oneself completely to God, and the stripping away of all personal pride and self-definition. After a long period of this kind of rigorous discipline (and others even more inventive), the mind, and therefore the soul, will be purified of the distractions of the ego, personal vanity, and even one's sense of identity.

In the end, all that will remain is the nameless human being stripped of all extraneous things, naked and humbled before God. It is in such a state while waiting for the manifestation of God that the darkness reveals itself, filling the monk with doubt, fear, terrible and tormenting visions and nightmares, hopelessness, and the despair of failure—of being unworthy. If it were not for the brief but overpowering experience of union with God that uplifts and transforms the monk, then this process would produce nothing but madness. However, it is a deliberative process and one that is voluntary.

From the standpoint of Christian mysticism, and even other forms of religious mysticism, this process is quite relevant and necessary to achieve spiritual maturity and the realization of the Spirit within oneself and transcending all matter. However, there would also be a corresponding negation of the material world and its various trials and tribulations. Overcoming the Dark Night of the Soul would at least confer on the mystical seeker a certain amount of freedom from the travails of the world since such a person would be functioning temporarily at a transcendent level of being. Such exalted states of consciousness are difficult to maintain, even for someone living a secluded life in a monastery, so the Dark Night would be something that would periodically recur, again and again. According to the various writings of Christian saints, including modern ones such as

Mother Teresa, the Dark Night of the Soul is an almost perpetual companion for the mystical seeker.

However, would such a process as the Dark Night of the Soul that I have described above be something that a Witch or Pagan might encounter if they were following an initiatory path within a Pagan-based system of ritual magic? That's an important question, and I believe that it is not part of the modern Witch or Pagan initiatory process. Why do I think that way? Is there a real distinction between the magical practitioner and the mystic? The answer, based solely on the cycle of transformative initiation, must be no. There are other possibilities, such as a Christian magician who is following a path that alternates between the paths of magician and a mystic. I would personally find this path confusing and perhaps even contradictory, but given the predilection that monotheistic religions have for antinomianism, it is possible.

If there is a possibility for darkness and despair, then it will be experienced when the Witch or Pagan Initiate is deep within the underworld, having experienced a complete shattering of the self into its most rudimentary parts. However, this period doesn't last long, and it is soon replaced with the opposite feelings of joy and illumination. In this case, the underworld serves as a cocoon preparing one for transformation. It is also possible that the Witch or Pagan Initiate could experience a kind of depression after having successfully completed a very difficult spiritual transformation as a kind of postpartum let-down after the fact—as if there should be something more. Yet even this state will not last long.

As you can see, the entire cycle of transformative initiation and its overarching purpose is to reintegrate the Initiate with a renewed self-image and sense of purpose in the mundane world. According to the creed of initiatory magic, the real work is to integrate spirit and matter, first within oneself, and then in the world at large. Accomplished Witches and Pagans are the teachers, initiators, leaders, and social transformers, using a combination of religion, science, and magic to change themselves and the world as a whole; to bring to fruition the cosmogonic design as coauthored by the Deities. In other words, to fulfill their own destiny and the destiny of the whole world simultaneously. That objective can't be fulfilled if the Initiate has renounced the material world. They must be immersed within it, but neither imprisoned nor corrupted by it.

Then there is the metaphorical beast of depression itself, and this is something that lies beyond the actual process of spiritual ascension or magical transformation. Whether the state of depression is situational or chronic, it can be quite a formidable opponent. People need to understand (if they don't already) that depression is a medical condition. Even if this is an individual and personal ordeal, it has greater social and even psychological implications. I would never recommend to anyone that they shouldn't seek out proper help when faced with an insurmountable and unresolvable problem. I, myself, cannot speak of depression as a chronic malady, although I have experienced it in a situational context from time to time.

However, there are many ways of dealing with the malady of depression, and the magician or mystic must deal with it (or any other psychological disorder) to achieve spiritual maturity. Chronic depression is a clinical disorder that can be mitigated with mood-altering drugs and/or lifestyle modifications to balance and enhance brain chemistry, but situational depression sometimes requires the ability to detach oneself to accurately assess one's situation and truly realize positive attributes of one's circumstance.

I really do believe that there is always a way or a path that can lead a person to a healthier and happier mental state, sometimes the difficulty is just finding it. I also have little pity for someone who persistently indulges in their internal pain and depression and doesn't seek any kind of help, counsel, or even some temporary diversion to drive the gloom from their mind. There is a stigma in our society that prejudges anyone who acknowledges psychological issues, so admitting them and seeking help can be intimidating. Still, this is one barrier that a person must overcome to find relief.[19]

Sometimes we just need a pep talk from someone outside of our situation to get us out of a slump, or perhaps some coaching to remind us that we do have resources and abilities to change our

---

19   You can find more information on chronic depression as a disease on the NAMI website here: https://www.nami.org/Support-Education/Video-Resource-Library/What-is-Depression

lives. A loved one can remind us of why we arc here, or even a beloved pet can do this when we are assailed by doubt and despair.[20] Still, we are not completely helpless, nor are we without any means at our command to change our lives in such a manner as to give us joy and happiness. This must be realized as an important truth to motivate us to find a solution.

Obviously, this is an exceedingly difficult condition to overcome, but it can be conquered. In fact, it must be conquered if we are going to achieve anything in our lives. That fact alone can often help someone overcome their situational depression since doing nothing will ultimately achieve nothing except prolong that dark and seemingly endless night. Break up your life patterns, try something new, get moving, and then see what happens. Often, having something important to do will help you forget that you are feeling blue.

As F. Scott Fitzgerald famously said in his book, *The Crack-up*, *"In a real dark night of the soul it is always three o'clock in the morning."*

PATHWAY OF SPIRITUAL ASCENSION
AND THE WAY OF WITCHCRAFT

This brings us to discuss the objective for undergoing transformative initiation, and that is to achieve a form of spiritual ascension. Since Witchcraft and Paganism are magical religious paths attuned to the material world and the spirit world as one worldview, the question must be asked, *"What is spiritual ascension?"* Is spiritual ascension even something that is relevant?

Because of the link between spirit and matter, any kind of ascension with Witchcraft must include both attributes simultaneously. A spiritual change must also be a material change, which means that transformations must help someone to be a better person. Since change is very difficult, if not often impossible, then experiencing a

---

20   In the event that the resources in your personal circle are not able to assist or are insufficient in mitigating depressive symptoms or other signs of mental illness, please don't hesitate to reach out for professional help from a licensed clinician. In a crisis situation, the support hotline 988 services all U.S. states and territories, and is free and available 24/7 for call or text.

profound internal psychological transformation that has spiritual and magical underpinnings will impact someone not only internally, but their material situation as well.

That doesn't mean that the process, once established and guiding the seeker through periodic transformations, will make them happy or help them win the lottery. Following the process makes things happen, and most of them benefit the seeker and their family and friends. What that cyclic process does is bestow wisdom, life knowledge, insights, and life path corrections that lead to greater fulfillment. As far as material wealth is concerned, it is a means to an end, but an end in itself. I have followed this path guided by my process for many decades, and while I have not become wealthy, I have become wise. It has been my perception that the Deities have something else in mind for the Witch or Pagan who has undergone their transformations. Their goal is to make the world a better place, to help those in need, aid and give consolation to the sick and the dying, and act as an agent of spiritual intervention in an often cruel and mindless world. They do these deeds through their adherents, and what better agent for a Deity to work through than one who has evolved a higher level of wisdom and insight than the average person?

Everything changes in the world, but some people learn, grow, and become better than they were previously. Nothing stops or ceases to change in the material world, so we should seek to learn, grow, and ultimately master our lives. If our foundation is built on periodic trials, transformations, visions, and realizations, then we can be assured that what we know and do is guided by something greater than ourselves. We become the agents of the Gods acting in the world to bring light to the darkness, compassion to a world of suffering, teaching, sharing knowledge, and bringing judgment based on experience to bear on the problems of others or upon ourselves.

As a Witch or Pagan practitioner, we cannot separate ourselves from the material world. Yet we can evolve and ascend to a higher perspective, where spirit and matter become one, and all things are connected. In my many decades of working magic, I experienced that place where everything converges and tasted the ecstasy that it delivers. It is a brief moment in the long toiling years of my life, but it is more significant than anything else I have ever experienced.

It gives me hope, clarity, and optimism, and it strengthens my faith in the Gods. It also has made me a better magical practitioner and helped me to build a materially comfortable life.

I have accepted the gifts of undergoing periodic transformations, but I know that I also have responsibilities to the people of my faith and that there is an associated cost that accompanies these gifts. I must never take them for granted or allow them to blind me to my own flaws and failings since potential misfortune is always at my side. I keep that thought in mind when I deal with others since nothing can keep us from experiencing tragedy or catastrophe.

CHAPTER TWO

HERO'S JOURNEY
AND THE COSMOGONIC CYCLE

*"It has always been the prime function of
mythology and rite to supply the symbols that
carry the human spirit forward..."*
JOSEPH CAMPBELL,
Hero with a Thousand Faces, p. 11

The cycle of transformative initiation is filled with archetypes and symbols that characterize the stages that a seeker passes through. These are the veritable symbols of transformation that act as signposts for the various stages, as well as triggers for the psychic manifestation of that stage. We have examined the transformative initiation process fully, and we have shown that it represents the phenomenon that makes a scripted initiation so powerful and compelling. Yet, this cycle is not a mystery to us, nor is it something that is outside of us, lurking in the shadows of consciousness. It is an intimate story plot that we all know and even celebrate in our culture, but one that resides in our minds and souls. This story is the Hero's Journey, and it can be realized as the Heroine's Journey as well.

The Hero's Journey has within it two processes. One is the cosmogonic cycle of the world or universe, and the other is the process of transformation that the hero undergoes to achieve rebirth into a new person or identity. We have discussed how the cyclic process of transformation is like the diurnal cycle of wakefulness and sleep, but that cycle is also imprinted on the cosmogonic cycle as well. The diurnal cycle of the sun as witnessed on the surface of the Earth was seen by many ancient people as the ascent and descent of the sun through underworld trials, to be reborn every morning from the decline and death at the close of the day of the previous evening. What they were doing was projecting their own diurnal cycle on the universe at large. We should briefly examine that mythic story since it is a part of the two cycles of the cosmos and the individual seeker.

Because the Earth was thought to be flat, the only way that the sun could set in the west and return rising in the east was if it somehow passed under the Earth during the night. The Egyptians developed a powerful myth about this underworld passage, and it was seen and even made into magical literature that would greatly aid the pharaoh in his quest for rebirth and eternal renewal. The daily cycle of the sun was compared to the very first day in the creation and the subsequent stages of ascension and decline that occurred afterward.

It was the way that the Egyptians saw the never-ending pattern of day and night and the changing seasons of the calendric cycle and compared them to a similar pattern of creation and dissolution of the cosmos. It allowed them to propose this cycle of life, death, and rebirth for their kings. Then it was only a short time when even commoners sought to appropriate this cycle once reserved only for the kings. Yet it was the Greeks later who made the cycle of the hero into an archetypal journey called by Joseph Campbell "the monomyth," even though every other person on the planet developed their own version.

The monomyth of the cyclic journey of the hero's descent into the underworld, undergoing many trials, and their ascent from out of it as a person renewed and reinvigorated was based on the cosmogonic cycle of the Earth itself. The four stages of creation, the golden age, the age of death, and the final dissolution, and their never-ending cycle around an unknowable and unlimited source became the example for the cycle of life, death, and rebirth of the individual mortal human being. Because death is the ultimate and unresolvable Mystery and crisis for all living beings, the prospect of rebirth, renewal, and regeneration has always been a powerful antidote for the depressing and pessimistic finality of life. The one exception is, of course, Buddhism, but that's another topic altogether.

The cosmogonic cycle has roughly four stages revolving around a monistic center that symbolizes the eternal source, that singularity where everything has its origin in the beginning and ends up returning in the end. The Hero's Journey has three basic thematic stages that cycle through the double gateway of the underworld, consisting of events that occur and lead up to before the passage, the ordeals and trials occurring during the passage, and then the trials of the return from that passage. A few scholars have proposed the fundamental number of stages for this hero's underworld journey, but it was Joseph Campbell who proposed a full seventeen stages that represent a universalized mythic structure.[21] The five-part cosmogonic cycle and the Hero's Journey together make for twenty-two stages.

Hero's Journey and the Fool's Journey

Many years ago, when I read Joseph Campbell's book *The Hero with a Thousand Faces*, I discovered that the exact number of Tarot trumps found in the Major Arcana was identical to the overall number of stages he had proposed for the Hero's Journey and the cosmogonic cycle. I also found that this apparent coincidence had an even greater importance when I was able to match each Tarot trump to one of these twenty-two stages. This wasn't a loose affiliation; the twenty-two stages matched the twenty-two Tarot trumps almost exactly. Yet I didn't so much use this newly discovered pattern as a tool for Tarot divination as I did for practical magical applications. I found that the magical use of the double gateway was the whole basis for the underworld cycle not only of the Hero's Journey but of the mysterious process of transformative initiation itself. I have employed this pattern using the western and eastern gateways as written in the magical workings of Witchcraft magic. You can find it in all four of my previous books.

The Hero's Journey was also the cyclic process of death and rebirth that ruled the more profound changes that occurred within a person's psyche. Also, since I used the sequence of the stages in the Hero's Journey to specifically qualify the matching Tarot trumps, it did indeed change how I defined those trumps, and it impacted how I interpreted them within a divinatory reading. But the Roman numerals that were printed at the very top of each Tarot trump seemed to have less to do with the actual sequence of the Hero's Journey and could therefore be ignored when working with this pattern.

---

21   Campbell, Joseph. *The Hero with a Thousand Faces*.

However, I found that the greatest power in using this structure was in the actual development of a Mystery system of the Self, which is one of the key elements in the five Mysteries of the modern Pagan world. Since the Mystery of death is one of the greatest Mysteries, along with the Mystery of the creation of life, any archetypal system that uncannily depicted that process would represent an immensely powerful symbology useful in both ceremonial initiations and magical workings.

This pattern consisting of accessing the underworld, experiencing a complete dissolution of the self and its resolution and return to unity in a new guise, and finally emerging from out of that place of darkness and death is perhaps the greatest Mystery cycle for all living things. It is also reminiscent of a more ancient psycho-spiritual cycle, which is the healing and redeeming cycle of the archetypal shaman. So, this archetypal pattern is not only very ancient, but it is still very relevant today. I have discovered that it is completely integral to any kind of modern Wiccan or Pagan system of magic and mystery.

Yet as I have proposed the universality and usefulness of this cycle of transformative initiation in the works of ritualized Mysteries and the basic tools of Witchcraft magic, others have also seen this analogy between the Hero's Journey and what is called the "Fool's Journey," or between the cycle of the hero and the sequence of the Tarot trumps as based on the Roman numerals. These others have included a few authors who have taken this pattern analogy and applied it strictly from the perspective of the Tarot and performing Tarot divination. Still, there is some question as to whether what I am proposing is a complete comparative analogy between the stages of the Hero's Journey and transformative initiation, and what others have called the myth of the Fool's Journey. They have reported that these two different cycles represent merely two different ways of stating the same thing.

As far as I am aware, the Fool's Journey is a title for the numeric sequence of the twenty-two trumps of the Tarot, beginning with the first card in that sequence, which is the Fool. Some writers have compared this sequence with the seventeen stages of Joseph Campbell's Hero's Journey, mostly using the stages as placeholders for a Tarot card reading using all seventy-eight cards.

However, the seventeen stages of the Hero's Journey do not represent the complete cycle because it is missing an important additional set of five stages, which are known as the "cosmogonic cycle," or the Cycle of Creation through Dissolution. The cosmogonic cycle is important because it represents the vision that the hero experiences when they are fully reconstituted (reborn) and rewarded with a boon or gift for their achievement. In fact, I will go as far as to say that the vision is synonymous with the boon that the hero receives. The critical importance of that vision of the cosmogonic cycle is that it assists the hero in determining their destiny within the greater world drama once they have acquired a renewed self-definition.

The cosmogonic cycle consists of the five basic phases of the material and spiritual universe. These are described by the five rubrics—Source, Creation-Emanation, Mythic-Golden Age, Age of Death, and Ultimate Dissolution. These five stages represent the life cycle of the cosmos, and it is important for the hero to realize their specific role and part in this transitional drama. So, the cosmogonic vision not only imparts the mythic narrative of creation and dissolution, but it also determines the specific mythic and historical context of the hero, showing their place in the present world and their ultimate destiny.

What I have proposed would essentially exclude any consideration of the Fool's Journey since by applying all twenty-two trumps to all the stages, including the cosmogonic cycle, the numeric sequence at the top of each card (typically in Roman numerals) is altogether ignored. Therefore, when examining the twenty-two Tarot trumps as active archetypes to be used within magical initiations and invocative operations, they become actual triggers for spiritual and psychic transformation. In other words, these twenty-two stages become the actual symbolic progression of a profound internal transformation which is harnessed and controlled by the magical practitioner. They function as the symbols of transformation for psychic transformation.

This is quite different than anything that I have so far seen where the Fool's Journey is compared to the Hero's Journey. What I am proposing has little to do with divination, other than it serves to completely redefine the Tarot trump cards when they appear in a reading. It has to do with dynamically using the Tarot trumps to trigger an internal, psychic, and spiritual transformation within the operator. It is, therefore, a highly active and instrumental use of this pattern.

Additionally, there is not only a Hero's Journey but also a Heroine's Journey. Although this mythic theme is rare, it does have some representations, most notably in the tale from antiquity entitled *Eros and Psyche*, which appeared in the book *The Golden Ass*, written by Apuleius. Another example of this myth is to be found in the Scandinavian folktale *East of the Sun and West of the Moon*. It can even be found in the modern story, *The Wizard of Oz*.[22] While like the Hero's Journey, it is also remarkably different, so it would have a somewhat different sequence of twenty-two trumps to effectively qualify that cycle. Thus, where a man might focus on the archetypal Hero's Journey, a woman might focus on the archetypal Heroine's Journey. Of course, the complexity of gender would cause these archetypal journeys to vary, they would also remain relativity intact because they represent our world culture at such a high mythic level.

As far as I know, I have not found anyone who has talked about the Fool's Journey and the Heroine's Journey, so that aspect of the magically transformative cycle for the archetypal feminine has yet to be adequately covered by an author.

Twenty-Two Stages of the Hero's Journey and the Tarot Trumps

Joseph Campbell's book *Hero with a Thousand Faces* is an examination of the mythic and literary Hero's Journey. In his version, there are twenty-two stages and four sections to this cyclic journey. There are three sections that are a specific part of the Hero's Journey, and one section that is the cosmogonic cycle. I can show that these two cycles are linked, so that would make the overall set of stages at twenty-two. It has the psychological quality and mythic motif of a journey into and out of the underworld with a corresponding world vision, which places it within the domain of the cultural collective mind. I read this book back while attending college, probably around forty-five years ago and it was profoundly revelatory.

---

22 Baum, L. Frank. *The Wizard of Oz*, George M. Hill Company, 1900.

What I discovered back then was that the trump cards of the Tarot fit the descriptions of the stages of the Hero's Journey quite amazingly well. You know how it is with curious minds, we see matching numbers of things and wonder if they are somehow related. That's what I did so many years ago. After reading over the stages, I took out my Crowley deck, separated the trump cards, and attempted to match them up with the twenty-two stages. I thought that this would be kind of difficult since I would have to ignore the Roman numerals at the top of each card, but instead, matching turned out to be quite easy. While I am certain that the cards and stages that I matched are quite solid, there could be some disagreements about this card or that, but an overall acceptance about trying to match them.

What you are seeking at this point is proof that the Tarot cards and stages of the Hero's Journey do match. Let us now start with an overview and then go through each stage in the Hero's Journey and World Vision and check if what I have selected as a match works.

The Heroic Cycle contains two actual opposing cycles: the hero's descent into the underworld and his return, and the cosmogonic cycle, which is the hero's vision of the creation and ultimate dissolution of the archetypal World/Universe.

There are eight basic milestones to the hero's underworld cycle of descent and return, these are encapsulated by the following stages.[23]

1. Call to adventure
2. Helpers and assistance
3. Threshold crossing—meeting the guardian
4. Minor trials and helpers
5. Supreme Ordeal (Sacred Marriage, Father Atonement, Apotheosis, Elixir/Boon, gift/theft)
6. Flight or release
7. Return threshold crossing
8. Elixir/Boon translation

---

23   Joseph Campbell, *Hero with a Thousand Faces*, p. 245.

The basic Hero's Journey.

Gaining the elixir, favor, or boon is the objective of the underworld transit—it is first and foremost the integration of the light and dark halves of the Self into a renewed and holistic individuation. It is also the revelation of the greater Cosmic Mystery—the passage of the ages of creation, the golden age, the age of death, and the final dissolution of the world, and more importantly, the hero's role within that cosmic and mythic history.

I will now present the twenty-two stages of the Hero's Journey and the cosmogonic cycle with the matching Tarot trumps. I will explain what the stage represents and how the Tarot card fits into that stage. For purposes of clarity, I have elected to use the Smith-Waite Tarot deck when examining the specific Tarot card images. In some cases, I have referred to the Thoth Tarot deck, since some of the card naming and symbology are a better fit for the comparison. I am also using my own distillations of Joseph Campbell's titles for each stage, adding text to help clarify them since this will help you to follow my matches and compare them to what Campbell has written in his book. The stage definitions and the trump card meanings are completely my own interpretations based on the Tarot card and Campbell's book.

PART I—THE SEPARATION OR DEPARTURE

1. The Summoning or Call to Adventure; the Revelation of the Vocation of the Hero (Trump: XX—The Last Judgment)

This is the first stage that represents the event or occasion when the normal mundane world is intruded upon or superseded by an event that presages the beginning of a mythic or supernatural process in the life of an individual or a society as a whole. For the hero, this event is symbolized by a herald or an announcement declaring that the time for momentous occasions is now at hand. This start of the heroic cycle can be subtle or dramatic, but it symbolizes that a certain event has brought forth a crisis and that nothing can either stop or overturn what has started.

The Last Judgment (XX) is the beginning of the end-times in the New Testament when the normal order of the mundane world has been overturned by powerful and irresistible supernatural forces set in motion by God to judge the world and all its inhabitants. The scene in the card is where the archangel Gabriel is blowing his horn to raise the dead from their graves. In Tarot readings, this card would represent a drastic and unexpected change that will bring both good fortune and bad fortune, depending on the fate of individuals and nations.

2. The Refusal of the Call; Folly or Internalization
(Trump: 0—The Fool)

Whenever there is an impending catastrophe and all the signs are pointing to it, there is a tendency to deny that it is happening. We see the warning signs, but we fail to believe and heed them. This action, of course, is the folly of being a human and seems to be our natural condition. It is probably why individuals have mentally or physically collapsed, or why nations or empires have quickly fallen when the right opportunities present themselves. Another way of perceiving this stage is that the calling has been momentarily internalized so that it may be fully grasped and acted upon in an intelligent manner. This second phase is what happens to the hero who appears to deny the calling but is deeply processing it.

The Fool (0) is the perfect representation of the refusal or the internalization of the call. The fact that the Fool continues his progress even though he is about to walk off a cliff exemplifies the whole nature of this stage: that the call is inevitable and unavoidable regardless of how one responds to it.

3. Supernatural Aid or Intervention;
Meeting the Spirit Guide
(Trump: II—The Priestess)

The pause in the journey caused by the hero—who has apparently either refused the call or is internally processing it—meets with a personage who is a representation of the positive forces of this impending change. It is the guide or the representative of the supernatural power that has triggered the catastrophic change who comes to interrupt the stalling or internal processing of the hero and helps them to realize what they must do at that moment. This guide or helper is met at other points along the journey who assists the hero in making the right choices and taking the right action.

The Priestess (II) in the Tarot symbolizes spiritual guidance and advice, she is the representative of the Deities and can speak and prophesize for them. As the guide on the Hero's Journey, she is the one who explains what is happening to the hero and how they can best take advantage of their situation. The High Priestess does indeed function as a guide in Tarot card readings.

4. Crossing the First Threshold;
Meeting the Fierce Guardian
(Trump: IX—The Hermit)

Once the static situation is broken by the guide, the hero proceeds to the next stage and comes before the gateway entrance to the underworld. Protecting this doorway is the guardian of the gateway, who functions as the counterpart to the guide. Gaining entrance to the underworld is the first of many ordeals that the hero must undergo, and it can be as simple as answering questions, solving a riddle, or realizing a basic self-truth, or it can be as arduous as undergoing a form of physical death or corporal punishment. To cross the threshold, the hero must surrender their entire concept of self, identity, family, avocation, everything. They enter the underworld completely bereft of a self-identity, a purpose, or a destiny. Everything that existed before has been erased, thereby making the hero ready to assume a whole new identity and destiny.

The Hermit (IX) stands in a dark place holding a lantern and shedding light into the darkness. He holds a staff of authority, which gives him the power to determine truth from falsehood, and the truthful and virtuous seekers from the deceitful and the delusional. The Hermit is therefore the perfect guardian who enacts the law of truth and virtue to force submission, penance, limitations, and discipline upon the seekers of truth. All of this is in accord with the guardian of the gateway in the Hero's Journey.

5. The Transition to the Other World; the Underworld
(Trump: XVI—The Blasted Tower)

The hero crosses the threshold gateway and submits to the ordeal that makes their passage possible. They are now without identity or destiny, like a nameless ghost wandering the underworld. Their world has been completely obliterated and only the darkness and the host of lost souls populate this domain. The underworld has many different symbolic representations. It can be Hades, Hell, or the belly of a giant creature, like the whale in the tale of Jonah. This place is cut off from the outside world and functions by its own set of rules, and the hero will need to master those rules to rediscover who they are, as well as their destiny.

The Blasted Tower or the House of God (XVI) is an emblem of the destruction of the old order and a reduction to the basic polarity of heaven and hell. A lightning bolt blasts a tower (like the Tower of Babel) throwing off a crown-like cupola and hurls nameless individuals from its battlement to the ground, while an earthquake opens to swallow the tower whole. This Tarot card depicts ruin, the overturning of law and order, and the complete disruption of ordinary life. Seen as the house of God, there is a theme of retribution and the punishment of arrogance and false pride. The house is destroyed by the supernatural force that helped to build it. Comparing this Tarot card with the stage in the Hero's Journey appears to fit with the idea of a hellish place where everything has been overturned.

PART II—THE TRIALS AND VICTORIES OF INITIATION

1. The Road of Trials; the Dangers and Lesser Ordeals (Trump: X—The Wheel of Fortune)

The hero undergoes a series of trials, all of them involving some kind of overcoming or escaping from the threat of death. These trials can be seen as a form of preparation for a greater and ultimate trial. The hero will likely find helpers who will assist them in overcoming each trial, and when the trial is completed, something precious is gained. Each completed trial informs the hero something about themself that they never previously knew, symbolizing that the hero is regaining parts of themself and starting to realize themself from a completely new and different perspective. The various helpers are, of course, aspects of the guide, who continue to help, guide, and instruct the hero as they navigate the hazards of the underworld.

The Wheel of Fortune (X) has a gambling wheel suspended in the sky, surrounded by the four archetypal beasts (four evangelists), where a sphinx stands upon its crest and a horned man is sliding off at its bottom. In a Tarot card reading, this card represents the ever-changing forces of fortune and that nothing remains unchanged. It can denote good fortune or bad, but it symbolizes that every rise is followed by a fall and that individuals should seek spiritual wisdom as a foundation instead of relying just on material fortune. How this trump card fits into the Hero's Journey is that the trials are like the trials of fortune and that the only way to achieve lasting success is through self-knowledge and the wisdom of the Gods. Every trial of life has something to teach us about ourselves that we didn't know previously, so the wheel would aptly represent the lesser trials of the underworld.

2. Meeting the Great Mother; Infancy Regained (Trump VI—The Lovers)

The hero encounters the supreme ordeal in the guise of a supernatural woman symbolized by the Great Mother. The hero has obtained various fragments of their own being while undergoing the lesser trials and now must integrate the light and darkness within themself to become whole and renewed once again. This supreme ordeal is symbolized by the *hieros gamos,* or "divine wedding" between the mortal hero and the divine Goddess of nature. It is through this process of joining and making themself whole that the hero once again becomes a person with an identity. What the hero lacks is a destiny, since they have succeeded in resolving the supreme ordeal, they now reside in an idyllic stasis, but not for long.

The Lovers (VI) shows a man and a woman standing naked before each other with an angel presiding above them as if to sanctify the perfect union between them. The sun is shining above them, and behind them are the two trees of the Garden of Eden, the Tree of Life and the Tree of the Knowledge of Good and Evil. This Tarot card represents the perfect joining of opposites, where Adam and Eve (as his rib) are merged again. It is curious that the gnostic definition of salvation was self-knowledge and joining the male and female into one being. When this card appears in a reading, it represents a joyous union (love fulfilled), but it is also a critical choice that will have profound consequences. I think that it is quite evident that this Tarot card easily fits into the corresponding stage of the Hero's Journey.

3. Woman as Temptress; Agony of Separation (Trump XI—Strength)

—formerly Trump VIII, but I will go with Crowley's sequence.

The idyllic paradise that the hero has been immersed in is also a trap because they must become an individual being without any attachments, just as a baby must learn to function and survive without the physical attachment to its mother. What is required to become an individual and self-determined person is the unleashing of the power of the will, which is the will to be fully defined. That use of willpower causes the separation of the light and darkness of the soul so that it can function in the world as an individual psychic being. Otherwise, to be forever immersed in the Goddess of nature is to function without conscious self-determination, to be like a thing of nature without a soul or a distinct personality. The separation is painful, the Great Mother may resist this impulse or even fight the hero, yet like a birth, it is necessary for the hero to become a distinct individual once again.

Strength (VIII) shows a woman gently forcing the jaws of a beast-like lion to open in her direction. She has a halo consisting of the sign of infinity and a flower wreath on her head. Flowers decorate her gown. This card symbolizes that gentle but persistent power will overcome the savage nature of the beast. The beast represents our animal nature, our passions, and our volatile emotions that can be destructive and deadly. The woman is a personification of our higher rational self that, through discipline, can keep these destructive emotions under control and directed toward constructive efforts. It is an analogy of human nature itself, showing that our inner beast must be conquered, not by force but by gentle and consistent urging. There can be pain and even a fight of sorts, but the strong will of the rational self will overcome the mindless beast. This card also represents the process of individuation and self-direction, for without self-governance and willpower, we will fail to achieve anything in life.

4. Expiation with the Father; Establishment of Inner Values
(Trump: XV—The Devil)

Having achieved wholeness, self-definition, and self-determination, the hero must meet the final challenge of the supreme ordeal, and that is taking upon themself the function, career, and responsibilities that go along with a renewed self. The hero must undergo the tasks of once again yoking themself to their responsibilities and their role as a person in the world. This is the stage in the Hero's Journey where they meet the Great Father and assume his role and responsibilities, thereby becoming him. Once the hero has achieved this final challenge, they are ready to know their place in the world and their ultimate destiny.

The Devil (XV) is the archetypal Satan with horns, wings, and claw-like feet crouching upon a block of stone like some kind of throne. He is depicted as Baphomet, with an inverted pentagram on his brow. He makes the sign of "as above and so below" with a torch in the descending hand (*coagula et solve*), and at his feet are a naked man and woman (like the Lover's card) wearing horns and chains loosely placed around their necks. The Devil is a controversial character who can be seen as a negative or a positive heroic personage. For the occultist, the Devil in this card is the initiator of the Mysteries of the underworld, and the man and woman are willing accomplices in this initiation. When this card appears in a reading, it represents the transition beyond good and evil through the artifice of diabolism. To embrace darkness and light within the self is to exercise one's will over them both. To know good from evil and to understand that the world is neither good nor evil requires a strong inner morality to navigate the world. Although unusual at first glance, the card of the Devil seems to fit this stage quite well.

5. Apotheosis; Self as Exalted Being
(Trump: I—The Magician)

Here the hero has met and successfully resolved all three challenges of the supreme ordeal. They have integrated and individuated themself, and have assumed the responsibilities and challenges of their role and position in life. Yet, what they lack at this moment is to know their place in the world and to strategically act on that knowledge. Here the hero has become something of a superhero, they have all the potential of the world at their command and only need to express their will and make it manifest. This is the apex of the underworld journey, where the hero becomes like a God, fully empowered and waiting for the vision that will fill their soul with purpose and establish their ultimate destiny.

The Magician (I) stands before an altar table where his elemental tools are placed. He is dressed in his sacred vestments with a serpent cingulum around his waist. He holds in his right hand a double-ended wand pointing up and his left hand is pointing with the index finger to the ground and there is an infinity sign above his head. There is a flower arbor above his head and a garden at his feet, consisting of lilies and roses, the emblem of purity and passion. This card, when it appears in a reading, signifies the ability to transform the material world through the arts of the spirit and the mind. The Magician depicted in this Tarot card is obviously a perfect personification of heroic apotheosis. There is no need for further explanation.

6. The Ultimate Boon; the Secret Knowledge of the Soul is Revealed. (Trump: VII—The Chariot)

Campbell defined the boon as an elixir of imperishable being, a substance or process that confers immortality on the hero. I had puzzled over this definition, trying to determine how the boon that gives immortality to the hero can be reconciled with the greater cosmogonic cycle. Fame and legend would seem to be the essential nature of the boon, and what greater fame or legend could be discovered than to know one's destiny and fulfill it? In the long chapter about this stage, Campbell references the *Tao Te Ching*, Chapter Sixteen,[24] which he believed represented the mindset of this stage of the Hero's Journey. The part of this section of the *Tao Te Ching* that inspired me to tie the boon to the cosmogonic cycle is to be found in the following text.

---

24   Campbell, Joseph, *The Hero with a Thousand Faces*, p. 189.

"The ten thousand things rise and fall while the Self watches their return.
They grow and flourish and then return to the source.
Returning to the source is stillness, which is the way [Tao] of nature.
The way of nature is unchanging.
Knowing constancy is insight.
...Being at one with the Tao is eternal.
And though the body dies, the Tao will never pass away." [25]

What I saw in this description of the self (as the hero) observing the rise and fall of the world (ten thousand things) gave me the idea that the boon is the vision of the cosmogonic cycle from the perspective of the source that never changes, the monistic One. Understanding the source or still-point that resides in the unchanging center of the universe is to understand the entire cyclic process and one's single point within it. That is, in my opinion, the foundation of the boon, which is the visionary experience of the universal cycle and the revelation of one's destiny within that cycle. The knowledge of personal destiny is the essential quality of indestructible existence.

Therefore, the final act of the hero is to gain the vision of the cosmogonic cycle and their place within it, which is their personal destiny. Such knowledge causes the actions of the individual who possesses it to be certain, supremely confident, and fully a master of themself. This is certainly the secret knowledge of the soul, and when it is revealed, everything becomes illuminated and clear to the beholder. This stage of the heroic journey shows the hero receiving their ultimate rewards for successfully overcoming and integrating all the challenges that they have faced. The vision of the cosmic cycle is powerful and profound, and the knowledge that places the hero within that vision is unlike anything else that they have ever beheld. Yet, like every penultimate event in one's life, it is all too brief and quickly fades. What is required is to find a way to take this great secret knowledge back into the mundane world and transform it, but that challenge will be the greatest one the hero must face in the Hero's Journey.

The Chariot (VII) shows a crowned heroic warrior wearing the elegant celestial armor of the grail knight and standing in a chariot

---

25   Feng, Gia Fu translated *Tao Te Ching*, Lao Tzu, Chapter Sixteen (no page numbers).

with a four-posted canopy of stars.[26] His coat of arms is on the front of the chariot, represented by a shield with a vertical wheel and axel surmounted by a winged disk. The chariot is pulled by a team of white and black sphinxes. It is supposed that in the chariot the grail itself resides, protected and hidden by the knight. The meaning of this card is that it represents great honors and responsibilities, with the heroic stage of the ultimate boon or secret knowledge of the soul.

PART III—THE COSMOGONIC CYCLE; THE VISION THAT IS THE HERO'S BOON

0. Omphalos; the Central Origin of All Things (Trump: XXI—The World)

The source of everything is the monist unity and singularity that resides at the center of the cosmos. It is the center point that never moves or changes, the One from which all things proceed and to which all things return in the end. It is the beginning and the end, and it is both within and without the cosmos. It is the ultimate Mystery.

The World (XXI) a wreath-like snake whose mouth consumes its tail forms an ellipse and is surrounded on four sides by the emblems of the four elements. Dancing within this ellipse is a hermaphrodite, whose body is partially veiled with a stole and who holds in both hands double-ended wands. This perfectly represents the central point and origin of the world.

1. Emanations; Emergence from the Void (Trump: XVII—The Star)

This stage in the Cosmogonic Cycle is represented by the mythic creation of the world from out of the chaotic void, where the stars in the airy heavens are fashioned and separated from the earth and the waters. The joining of Earth and Water, aligned with the Fire in

---

26 In Crowley's version of this Tarot card, the heroic warrior is completely visored, and he holds in his lap the Holy Grail, which is an even more explicit depiction of the boon as the grail that transmutes matter into spirit, and spirit into matter.

the underworld, produces all the life in the world through a constant process of creation and emanation.

The Star (XVII) depicts a naked woman (Aquarius) kneeling between the waters of a lake and the grassy earth with her foot in the lake and her knee upon the earth, pouring a beaker of water into the lake and simultaneously on the earth. Above is an arc of seven stars and within its center is a great eight-pointed star. A great tree is on a hill in the background and farther out, a mountain. The typical interpretation of this card is healing, regeneration, and renewal. It would seem to represent cosmic creation in a kind of symbolic guise.

2. Virgin Birth; Creative Roles of Women and the Mythical Golden Age (Trump: III—The Empress)

The first age after creation is the notable golden age where all creatures lived in harmony and death and disease was unknown. There were heroic Gods and Goddesses who performed astonishing tasks, formulating the world as we know it today. It was a place of eternal peace and prosperity, where the function of creativity and the role of the archetypal woman reigned supreme overall. Yet, like all perfect worlds, it was destined to fail or to be divided with part of it cast off or warded, like the Garden of Eden. It is also typical that the role of men was to destroy this world and then try to seek and find it forever without success. It is like the age of an idyllic childhood that seems endless but must end at some time for the world to move and progress and for failure to be realized.

The Empress (III) sits upon a throne-like couch with a shield showing the sign of Venus at her feet. She is dressed in flowing robes adorned with the embroidery of roses. She wears a jeweled crown and holds a wand with an orb raised in her right hand as a symbol of her sovereignty. At her feet, around her dais, are stalks of grain, and behind her is a beautiful, wooded park. This card in a reading represents wealth, ownership, and gentle authority (a kind and compassionate leader), and it also represents a fortunate partnership. I think the meaning of this card fits the stage of the golden age of the cosmogonic cycle quite well.

3. Transformation; the Age of Death and Suffering
(Trump: XIII—Death)

With the fall of the Golden Age of Heroes and Gods comes the age of man, mortality, disease, and the misfortunes and calamities of material existence. The king and Deity of this domain is the spirit of death and the lord of the apocalypse. Of course, not everything is bad, and certainly, there is joy, happiness, and good fortune, but it is all too brief, and death takes away everything except the sorrow and disappointment of a fleeting and ephemeral existence.

Death (XIII) the card of Death shows the angel of death seated upon a pale horse dressed in black armor. The visor is open showing a grinning skull. He holds a pennant that has a white rose on a black field. Standing before him is a bishop praying for mercy, and around him are the bodies of a king, a child, and a woman. When this card appears in a reading, it can mean death, but usually, it means a profound and total transformation, which is another way of saying death. No need to compare this to the cosmogonic cycle—they match perfectly.

4. Dissolutions; the End of the World
(Trump: XII—The Hanged Man)

The final stage in the cosmogonic cycle is the end of the material and spiritual world—the final supreme transformation where everything returns and is dissolved into the One. While this ending may seem final, it is but the preparation for a renewed creation of a new universe. It is both the end and the moment just before the beginning.

The Hanged Man (XII) is a card that does not depict an execution, it is an initiation and a preparation for a future rebirth. It depicts a hallowed man hanging upside down by the right leg while the left is tucked behind at a forty-five-degree angle, forming the Hebrew letter *Mim* (water). He is hanging from two crosstrees forming a tau cross and these trees still have green leaves. This Tarot card symbolizes the ordeal of spiritual transformation (like baptism) and is therefore a form of death and rebirth. This card is a little less obvious when I attempt to compare it to the Cosmogonic Cycle of Dissolution and Endings. However, I think that the idea of death and rebirth is succinctly represented in both the cycle stage and the Tarot card.

PART IV—THE RETURN AND REINTEGRATION WITH SOCIETY

1. The Refusal to Return; the World Denied, the Completion of the Path of the Mystic (Trump: VIII—Justice)

—formerly Trump XI, but I will go with Crowley's sequence.

One of two possibilities in the Hero's Journey is that the hero will refuse to return to the material world after having achieved everything in the underworld, which is now their sovereign domain. They may choose to remain in this timeless and unchanging world and eternally enjoy the rewards of their greatness. However, because the hero now has the secret knowledge of their destiny, it is unlikely that they would be able to resist returning to claim that heritage which would only be given to them. The refusal of the return is also symbolized by the mystical renunciation of the material world, where there is no possibility of return. Once grace or enlightenment is achieved, there is a desire to keep this great gift and to share it with no one if a person subscribes to the path of mysticism.

Justice (VIII) represents order and equilibrium. It shows a crowned woman sitting on a throne between two pillars (like the Priestess) on a dais holding a sword pointed up in her right hand and a pair of scales in her left hand. There is a crimson veil behind her. Crowley called this card "Adjustment" instead of Justice, but I believe that it symbolizes the cautious and steady requirement for balance and equilibrium in all transactions. This desire for stability and balance could match the heroic stage of the refusal to return since to take any action would be to cause an imbalance. Maintaining order and balance would require no change or movement.

2. The Magic Flight;
Escape/Crossing the Return Threshold
(Trump: XVIII—The Moon)

If the hero seeks to return to the material world bearing their secret knowledge and treasure, then one of two things will happen. They will meet resistance, or they will be gracefully allowed to leave. In either case, they will have to travel to the crossroads threshold once again and there they will meet the guardian, the guide, and undergo the ordeal. Instead of being stripped of their identity, they will have to figure out how to translate what they have achieved in the underworld into a language or media that is intelligible to those who are outside their inner world. This process of translation will devalue or even greatly reduce the boon or treasure that the hero is seeking to take with them into the outer world. They may have been a superhero in the inner world, but they are just a person in the outer world, and they must figure out a way to transfer as much of that treasure as they can so it will help them in the outer world.

The Moon (XVII) depicts a winding pathway between two towers during the night of a full moon. The moon has a face that is frowning, and light shines from it, not as a blessing but more like a curse. The path starts at the shore of a lake where a crayfish is emerging from the water. On the left side of the winding path is a dog and on the right side is a wolf, both are howling at the moon. This card typically means betrayal, hidden enemies, plots, or a difficult path to freedom represented by the winding and twisting path. However, the two towers on either side of the winding pathway look a lot like how I would envision a return gateway from the perspective of the underworld, so I think that this card and stage are an obvious match.

3. Rescue from Without; the Healing of the Fisher King
(Trump: IV—The Emperor)

Sometimes the hero will have difficulties in making the transition from the inner world to the outer world, and they will need some kind of external intervention. Additionally, the hero might be trapped in the underworld and require an external authority to command the forces to allow their passage to the waking world. This stage is also symbolized by the Fisher King, who is mortally wounded but never dies. They are redeemed when the grail knight asks the question about the grail of life, the plate of ever abundance, the bleeding lance, and the sword of power to the congregants of the sacred feast. Failure to ask the question about whom the grail serves, where it comes from, and where it will reappear next dooms the quest until the grail appears again, many long difficult years later. Healing the Fisher King occurs only when the outer objective reality is successfully integrated with the internal spiritual truth.

The Emperor (IV) depicts a crowned and bearded sovereign sitting upon a throne and dais, wearing purple vestments over armor. He holds in his right hand a wand shaped like a tau cross with a ring affixed to it and an orb in his left hand. There are ram head sculptures on the armrests and on each corner of the top of the throne. The meaning of this card is authority, force, order, enforced peace, decisive leadership, and preparedness; it can also signify tyranny, inflexibility, and authoritarianism. While this Tarot card might represent the authority to rescue the hero from their inner world, it doesn't work with the mythic idea of the Fisher King. However, Crowley switches the Qabalistic Hebrew letters for this card and the Star, so instead of *Heh*, the letter for the Emperor would be *Tzaddi*, which in Hebrew is "a fishhook." Hence, the Fisher King.

4. The Reoccurrence of the Boon; the Expression of the World Redeeming Vision (Trump: XIV—Temperance)

Having finally crossed the threshold from the underworld into the outer waking world, the hero begins the next and final challenge of the Hero's Journey, and that is translating the secret knowledge they gained through their apotheosis and resultant cosmogonic vision into a knowledge that it is understandable and intelligible to the people in the waking world. They use mythology, art, music, and poetry, along with any and every other media to communicate what they have learned, both about themself and their destiny, to the world at large. They do this like any messenger of the Gods, by bringing myth and ritual into the waking world. While their renewed self and sense of purpose and destiny were at a monumental level within the underworld, these ideals are diminished and reduced to a more terrestrial level when they become intelligible in the material world. They still resonate with the mystery and power of the Otherworld.

Temperance (XIV) shows a winged angel wearing a white robe with a golden triangle of fire on it standing before a lake with one foot in the water and the other on the shore. She is pouring liquid from one golden chalice into another that she holds before her. She wears a diadem with the symbol of the sun etched on it, and a path winds from the lake to a mountain pass, where the sun is rising. Orchids grow to her left side. This card symbolizes the alchemical process of deriving the Universal Medicine through the fusion of opposites. It is more clearly depicted in Crowley's trump card named Art. I believe that the depiction of this Tarot card does match the heroic stage, although Crowley's version is probably better at showing that.

5. Master of Two Worlds; the Key to the Inner and Outer Realities (Trump V—The Hierophant)

When the challenge of translation is completed, the hero becomes, for a time, a master of both the inner and outer worlds. This is because they have accomplished the ability to readily translate the inspirations and ideations of the underworld into the language and rites of the material world. This skill represents a high degree of mastery, especially if they have managed to translate their vision and perspective without losing much of its internal psychic power and meaningfulness. They have become a conduit between the spirit and the material worlds and are able to powerfully influence both. Great teachers and infamous shamans had this ability, and it is a sign of greatness to be able to easily pass between both worlds.

The Hierophant (V) used to be called the Pope, but this depiction retains its meaning whether he is shown as the Pope or as a Hierophant of the Mysteries. The real significance of this card is that the Pope or Hierophant is always shown to have in his possession the twin keys of the spiritual and material worlds, where he is the master of both. I think, without a doubt, that this card matches the heroic stage. The meanings between the stage and the card are similar as well.

6. Freedom to Live; the Function of the Ultimate Boon (Trump: XIX—The Sun)

Mastery of the inner and outer worlds confers upon the hero a final accolade and reward; they can live a completely free and unencumbered life. All treasures and happiness are theirs to claim, but due to their wisdom, they choose to possess little and to live a simple life, fully, freely, and without fear. The period of idyllic and happy existence is temporary. Life is all about change, and anyone who rests on their laurels too long will experience the tragedy of life in some way or another. Even with all their accomplishments, the hero is still mortal and subject to physical and mental decline. Yet, for a short period of time, they have achieved all that can be achieved, and the only thing left to do is to live fully and feel deeply.

The Sun (XIX) depicts a naked child riding on the back of a silver horse in a sumptuous walled garden. His head is adorned with flowers, and he holds a beautiful, long, rose-colored silk pennant. The wall has golden sunflowers growing along the top and the sun, with a noble face, shines down upon the garden. This card means material happiness and fulfillment, but I can also perceive it to mean freedom and the joy of deliverance, making it a good match for the final heroic stage.

TAROT TRUMPS AND THE CYCLE OF INITIATION

These are the twenty-two stages of the Hero's Journey and the cosmogonic cycle as they are matched up with the twenty-two trumps of the Major Arcana. This cycle is also an emblem of the transformative cycle of initiation housing the symbols of transformation, thereby making it one of the most powerful magical tools in your magical toolbox. The Tarot trumps, now defined as stages in the initiation cycle, can be used to help you determine your initiatory stage or to trigger a particular stage that you need to occur.

This brings me to explain that there is the archetypal cycle of initiation, and then there is the initiation cycle that each and every one of us on the path is engaging in. The archetypal initiation is the whole twenty-two stages, but our personal initiation cycle is at one of the stages, perhaps waiting for the next trigger event before it will move on to the next stage. Our initiation starts when we experience a traumatic event in our lives, or perhaps even when we are initiated into a coven.

Transformative initiation is ongoing and ever-occurring. Once it starts, it will continue to cycle in an ever-widening spiral of spiritual evolution and life-based expansion. Sometimes it is slow, or even quiet, and other times it is quick, dramatic, joyful, painful, and obvious. Learning to master this cycle begins with identifying it within yourself, and then learning how to trigger aspects of it so it will have less of a painful effect. Getting stuck in a particular stage can be painful and difficult. We saw that some of the stages that occur in the underworld are very unpleasant but quickly resolved into the next stage in the archetypal cycle. Yet, in the real personal initiation cycle, a person might stay in a particular stage for months or even years, suffering through the entire process and not knowing why.

To determine where we are in the initiatory process, or to work a form of magic to hasten or push an initiatory stage, we will need a new ritual to help us make that determination. I will spend chapter four discussing this ritual and how to use it in both a passive divinatory way and in an active and magical way.

The twenty-two paths circle and the central pentagram.

CHAPTER THREE

HEROINE'S JOURNEY AND THE FEMININE INITIATION CYCLE

"Magic happens on the threshold of the forbidden."
MARIA TATAR

The Hero's Journey is a particularly archetypal masculine story, and it does not address that there is a whole other side to that cyclic process of transformation that would be about the archetypal feminine story of the Heroine's Journey. While these two cyclic processes differ, particularly in their literary adaption, the Hero's Journey is not exclusive to men, nor is the Heroine's Journey exclusive to women. They differ startlingly in their objective and outcome.

Examples of the Hero's Journey in modern media would be both the *Star Wars* series, *Episode IV, A New Hope* (1977), and the *Wonder Woman* movie (2017), to mention a few of the myriad of examples. Both films exemplify the Hero's Journey. However, examples of the Heroine's Journey are now almost as frequently represented by media storylines, such as the *Harry Potter* series or the *Twilight* series.[27]

Joseph Campbell, true to his gender and era, did not think that a woman had a true transformational journey, other than to evolve from Maiden to Mother and to give birth to children.[28] He apparently ignored the handful of myths and fairy tales that detailed the stages of this kind of transformative cycle, such as the classic

---

27 Carriger, Gail, *The Heroine's Journey*, p. 18.
28 Tatar, Maria, *The Heroine with 1,001 Faces*, p. 2.

tale of Eros and Psyche, which was contained in the book *Golden Ass* written by Apuleius in the second century. Also, the mythic stories of Demeter and Persephone (Greek), Isis and Osiris (Egyptian), and Inanna (Sumerian) are examples of the mythic Heroine Journey, except that in those cases, it is undergone by Goddesses instead of mortal women. This small fact probably excluded them from Campbell's consideration, but they show the antiquity of the Heroine's Journey.

There are other fairy tales as well, such as my favorite, the Scandinavian tale of *East of the Sun and West of the Moon,* and the Romanian folktale, *The Enchanted Pig.* Vestiges of this story are not to be found in the classical myths of the Greek and Roman Heroes, nor is it found in any of the other great cultural myths, so it is likely for this reason that Campbell did not address the theme of the Heroine's Journey. That omission followed a pattern of taking away the voices of the many women in the classical and mythic stories to be found in cultures worldwide, as we shall see.

The basic structure of the Heroine's Journey is that it is started by an involuntary loss or separation from the family and its social structure, which places the protagonist in a dangerous predicament. The Heroine's Journey is the search for a new social network and personal meaningfulness, where what was removed or broken is restored through negotiation and compromise and the help and assistance of others. It is a story of restoration, social justice (righting wrongs), and the rebuilding of the social world for the betterment of everyone. This story ultimately seeks balance and compromise.

If we examine the stages of this story with the journey of the psyche through disruption, fall, and reintegration, it represents a full restoration—a complete healing. The Heroine's Journey requires the interplay of others and is resolved through negotiation, reintegration, and compromise. The Hero's Journey is more isolated and solitary, although there are helpers at the very beginning (mentor or teacher), the hero must find their own way with little or no guidance. The path of the hero is lonely and truly dark and can more likely end with a potential failure than with a successful outcome. It also makes the reintegration after the return much more difficult after the underworld sequence has been completed since there is only the hero and whatever boon they have achieved to help them return to the mundane world. Often, that return is likely incomplete, making the hero someone who is outside of society and no longer a member of it.

Therefore, the Hero's Journey is darker and more dangerous, while the Heroine's Journey is not experienced alone and without helpers, friends, and social allies. The underworld sequence is often not as dire because it is not experienced without help and assistance from others. However, the purpose of the Hero's Journey in terms of the cycle of initiation is that the target for transformation is the one undergoing it, and the purpose of the Heroine's Journey is to change and redeem the world itself.

Sometimes, an individual may undergo the Hero's Journey to resolve a powerful or even disabling internal issue, and other times, they may undergo the Heroine's Journey to correct victimizations resulting from occurrences in the outer world and then take actions to externally change them. The darker and more extreme Hero's Journey represents a transformation of the self that is redeemed by a vision or a powerful realization (the boon), but the lighter, yet no less challenging Heroine's Journey represents the combined transformation of the self and the world at large. There is no vision or boon delivered in the Heroine's Journey, except the means to change oneself and, when necessary, redeem society.[29] There is also no fame, archetypal combat, victory, or glory in the Heroine's Journey since negotiation and compromise are the means through which it is resolved. While that might make the Heroine's Journey less sensational, its overarching accomplishment is often far greater and longer lasting than that of the Hero's Journey.

As I have stated, the Heroine's Journey lacks the vision of the cosmogonic cycle. However, that cycle is always present and a determinant of the character and quality of the Heroine's Journey. There is no doubt that women's place in the world is rapidly changing and evolving, and their place in society even a hundred years ago was

---

29   Carriger, Gail, *The Heroine's Journey*, p. 57–58.

quite different than it is now. The cosmogonic stages always show the greater cycle of change and evolution that occurs on a mythic level to the world at large, showing the ages of development from the beginning of time until the end of time, and highlighting the great epochs that occurred between them.

Heroine's Cycle.

While the Hero's cosmogonic cycle is spiritual and material based on technology (ages of gold, bronze, and iron) and the fall from the highest to the lowest spiritual and moral levels, the cosmogonic cycle of the heroine represents the socioeconomic stages of survival, egalitarian freedom, subjugation and domination, and a return to an enlightened egalitarian state of personal freedom. This kind of cosmogonic cycle is more like a never-ending spiral of spiritual and social evolution than it is a fall from grace where redemption is required for any kind of return.

We should, therefore, examine the cosmogonic cycle of the Heroine's Journey first before we delve into the cycle of the individual. This is because the macrocosmic cycle is a determinant of the microcosmic journey of the individual. We will also use the twenty-two trumps to characterize the stages of both the cosmogonic cycle and the individual cycle as we did with the Hero's Journey. Since we have done an extensive deep dive into the meaning of the trump cards as to how they pertain to the Hero's Cycle, I feel that we don't need to do such an analysis of the Heroine's Cycle. I will, however, seek to explain the differences and overarching themes that differentiate the two cycles.

The Heroine's Journey or initiatory cycle is broken into four parts, just as it is with the Hero's Journey. The first part is the cosmogonic mythic stages that represent the progression of our social and economic world from its infancy to its ultimate destiny. I have named the cosmogonic cycle for the Heroine's Journey "the Body of Woman as Avatar" since it is a procreative and nurturing cycle, representing humankind's socio-economic evolution, centered as it is on the role of women through the stages of human development. The actual Heroine's Journey has three parts, and these are called "Marriage to Death and the Serpent's Temptation," the "Trials of Love," and the final resolution, named "Daughter as Mother." Each of these three sections is distilled from the myth of Eros and Psyche, as well as the myths of Demeter, Isis, and Inanna. Each of these mythic cycles is different, but each retains an element of Descent, Search, and Ascent elements of the literary Heroine's Journey. I have added my creative perspective on them and used the trumps to illustrate my rendition of this initiatory cycle.

BODY OF WOMAN AS AVATAR—
THE VISIONARY MYSTERY

The cosmogonic cycle of the Heroine's Journey illustrates the age-old cycle of the mythic battle between the sexes and the changes that this contest wrought on the various ages and stages of human development. However, this is from the perspective of women, who are the makers and shapers of life, and whose ministrations, discoveries, and teachings have represented a world where human activity is in balance with nature as its natural expression. Of course, there is conflict within this worldview, and there are times of imbalance, subjugation, oppression, and dominance. Still, the power of negotiation, the moral arc of justice, and the movement toward greater equity and social unity fulfill the cycle with a return to balance and harmony within a greater cultural maturity.

The cosmogonic cycle begins with the Tarot trump the World/ Universe (XXI) as the source of all that is and will be. From that point, it differs from the hero's cosmogonic cycle.

Emanations and the golden age stages are represented by the Tarot trumps the Chariot (VII) and the Sun (XIX), characterizing the formative period of humanities ascent with the power of life as the grail of procreation and provender, which allows for an egalitarian lifestyle of equity and social unity. The Sun Tarot trump represents life in a garden of balanced existence, where survival has been fully established and the earth is the breadbasket of bounteous gathering, animal husbandry, and sporadic agriculture.

Through these two stages, the focus is on the role of women in society and their power of giving and shaping life. From the Stone Age to the Neolithic, most societies experimented with different social organizations, but within these social arrangements, clan membership and kinship determined the distribution of gathered and crafted goods. While hunting may have added much-needed protein to the diet of early humanity, the dominance of social networks by male-lead hunters was not a significant element of human culture until later.

Inequality, therefore, had its origin in the cultural dominance of men, as warriors and hunters, who amassed a greater share of goods as their right of rulership. This stage is represented by the Tarot trump the Emperor (IV), characterizing an age of oligarchy based on conquest, spoilation, suppression, and control. Even when city-states chose monarchs to rule over them in the early stages of the Bronze Age, these rulers only had power vested in them by a council of elders who could remove and replace them if they chose to do so. However, that early period was followed by warrior elite and monarchs who ruled empires and who took a greater share of wealth and power, leaving those deemed of a lesser value or status with a meager existence.

The final stage in this five-part cyclic process is when the static, hierarchical, and patriarchal social structures begin to break down and fail, due in no small part to the influences of a greater democratization of the social and institutional organizations. As the ruling class must allow and include a greater share of the population, then that ruling class will fall and be overcome by a new social consensus—democratic rule. The Tarot trump that characterizes this age is the Star (XVII), which manifests first as hope, optimism, and a belief in the possibilities of change. This is a time of social justice, where inequality is overthrown and individual freedom is balanced by the obligations of self-determination and social alignment. This is a time for unification, healing, restitution, and equal justice—rights for all living beings. Harmony and balance are restored, as they once were, but at a higher and more evolved level.

As you can see from my description of the mythic stages from the perspective of the archetypal feminine, we are still in the age characterized by the Emperor. While much progress has been made, there is a period of regression that has also occurred, but ultimately, this evolving progress will enable our world to assume greater liberty and an escape from inequality through a more democratic and inclusive society.

HEROINE CYCLE STAGE ONE— MARRIAGE TO DEATH AND THE SERPENT'S TEMPTATION

The first three stages in the Heroine's Cycle are the same as they are in the Hero's Cycle since the cycle is triggered by some kind of call, which is refused or internalized, to be followed by some kind of intervention. The intervention in the Hero's Cycle is nearly always voluntary, brought about by the introduction of a mentor or teacher who acts as his guide. For the heroine, however, the intervention is involuntary, representing the fact that her change in social status often was abrupt, chosen without her consent, and unwanted. So, despite this difference, the Tarot trumps of the Last Judgement (XX), the Fool (0), and the Priestess (II) represent the first part of the descending stage of the cycle of the hero and the heroine.

The themes of death and temptation occur in the Heroine's Cycle from the trump cards of the Lovers (VI) and Death (XIII), respectively. The death theme represents the change in the state of the maiden to the married woman, where one life and its family relationships are given up and lost as the newly-wed woman assumes her role with her husband in a new family. Joining with its promise of renewal and reintegration is shown to be illusory since the wife now becomes the property and dominated partner of a patriarchal social structure. Whatever dreams or aspirations she might have had, she now must conform to a new order where she is subordinate and expected to be fertile and fruitful. This is the archetypal descent that is represented by loss and separation but inspires a renewed search. Her loss of identity forces her to assume a new identity as a form of disguise, and her work is to subvert, however modest, the existing social regime.

In the myth of Psyche, her family is ordered by an oracle to imprison her on a mountain so that only some terrible monster will claim her as a wife.[30] She has a wedding that is a funeral, and her hand is reluctantly given to death by her parents. Aphrodite, who is jealous of Psyche's beauty and charm, seeks to destroy her. But when her son, Eros, goes to the mountaintop to complete the binding to death, he falls in love with her. He releases her but takes her to his secret place where she must swear complete obedience and not allow her curiosity to probe into the identity of Eros or his godlike work.

A similar trope is found in the fairy tale *East of the Sun and West of the Moon*, where the youngest daughter of a poor woodcutter is given to a bear as her husband for a bag of gold.[31] Although she lives in a sumptuous palace, she is sworn to do nothing to reveal her husband's identity when he comes to her by night and then changes into a handsome prince. The nature of curiosity and the desire to know are the temptations that drive her to break her vow and reveal the face of her mysterious husband, which breaks the spell and leaves her

---

30 Johnson, Robert A., *She—Understanding Feminine Psychology*, p. 11–13.

31 Willard, Nancy, *East of the Sun and West of the Moon*, p. 13–14.

without either the palace or the changeling spouse. To restore what she has lost, she must travel to an island castle that is *East of the Sun and West of the Moon*, a seemingly impossible feat, but made possible with the assistance of her allies and helpers.

HEROINE CYCLE STAGE TWO— TRIALS OF LOVE AND RESTORATION

Like the hero, the heroine undergoes trials to rebuild what she has lost and to prove that she is worthy of that restoration. These trials can occur along with an underworld visitation, or the entire process, once past the marriage of death, occurs in the archetypal conscious reality of the underworld.

The very first stage is the same in the Hero's and Heroine's Cycle, and that is characterized by the Tarot trump the Wheel of Fortune (X). The lesser trials always symbolize the steps that one must take to be challenged and proven worthy, where typically failure is a form of death. While the hero undergoes these challenges without any help or assistance because they are completely isolated, the heroine faces them always with guides, helpers, and surrogates who can even perform the deeds for her. The fact that she has these allies who can help her accomplish these trials is the very thing that shows she is worthy.

The lesser trials are followed by the supreme ordeal in both cycles, yet here the supreme ordeal for the heroine is the inverse of what the hero must face. The hero must overcome the temptation of the mother and atone with the father to achieve self-reintegration. The heroine must overcome her father to find her power and self-determination. Here, the father is characterized as the negative attribution of the male-dominated patriarchal system. The supreme ordeal is defined by the Tarot trumps of the Devil (XV) and Strength (XI). These two trump cards represent the ultimate contest between evil and good, but unlike the Hero's Cycle, neither evil nor good is the focus of the challenge, but the way that they are defined structurally allows them to be integrated into a combined mythic archetype where the light and darkness are blended and merged into one.

Still, for the heroine, achieving self-determination and overcoming the negative aspects of masculinity is only the first part of this ordeal.

157

There are also the trump cards Justice (VIII) and the Hanged Man (XII), representing the process of negotiation and self-sacrifice or compromise, required to fully restore the heroine to her social status from an inner perspective. The outcome of this process is characterized by the Tarot trump Temperance (XIV), which represents the heroine's ability to reconnect and reintegrate within a new social framework. The result of the supreme ordeal is a restoration of balance and harmony.

Keep in mind that at this point in the Heroine's Cycle, what she has achieved is internalized and based on her individual situation. It is all in her mind, but that is where it must be first realized. To truly apprehend this renewal in the mundane world, she still must undergo a process where that inner perspective is united with the outward social reality.

With the myth of Psyche, she must undergo four trials that her mother-in-law, Aphrodite, has challenged her to complete or face certain death.[32] She has helpers who aid her in meeting three of the challenges, but the fourth is where she fails. After retrieving a jar of ointment from Persephone in Hades during an exchange of gifts, she opens it before giving it to Aphrodite which causes her to die. Still, Eros seeks permission from the Gods and restores Psyche to life and then marries her in Olympus, where she gives birth to a daughter, named Pleasure.

HEROINE CYCLE STAGE THREE— ASCENT: DAUGHTER AS MOTHER

The transformation of the heroine occurs when she returns from her involuntary exile to assume her role as the arbiter and judge of the mundane world with its inequalities, strife, victimization, and exploitation. She has achieved an inner sense of empowerment and strength, but now she must act to mitigate what has victimized her personally, as well as make the world a better place when that state of justice is brought to realization. She now moves with purpose and with destiny because she has managed to build a new social network and can, through its agency, address the inequalities that forced her to abdicate. The old social order is gone, but it has now been replaced by a better and stronger one.

---

32 Johnson, Robert A., *She—Understanding Feminine Psychology*, p. 47.

In the Heroine's Cycle of Ascent, the first stage that she encounters is characterized by the Tarot trump the Tower (XVI), which represents the old order that is tottering and decaying, and only needs a push to send it crashing down. In this case, the Tower does not represent the entirety of the patriarchal world, but only a part of it that has concerned the heroine from her beginning descent. She has the strength and resources to face this issue since it no longer has the power to oppress or subjugate her. Her return is the lightning flash that overturns the old order, but that is only the beginning of her challenges.

Every step of progress in the ever-turning cycle of equality and justice often has counterforces or a backlash that seeks to kill that change before it becomes a normal part of the social structure. This stage of the ascent is characterized by secret plotting and betrayals, often instigated by those who pretend to be allies and staunch supporters. When change happens in a society, it is resisted not only by those who may lose their dominance but those who are comfortable with the status quo and fear what might occur when changes are wrought. Betrayal, secret plotting, and intrigues are fitting qualities for the Tarot trump the Moon (XVIII), and the heroine must deal with these backlashes with steadfast and persistent action. Only in this manner will she be able to progress to the next stage.

The next three stages of the ascent represent the breakthrough agreement, internalization of the process, and a final externalization, where justice and equality, restoration and reunion are achieved through consensus and compromise. The three stages are characterized by the Tarot trumps of the Empress (III), the Hermit (IX), and the Hierophant (V). The Empress is the realization of the daughter as a mother, where she becomes the author in fact of the new order. The Hermit and the Hierophant show that there should be a period of reflection and internalization to fully comprehend and engage with the achievement, to be followed by a period of the assumption of the new role that such an achievement demands. A social change must be shepherded to prevent any kind of relapse, and the role of the Hierophant symbolizes that process where the internal and external worlds meet in a harmonious union.

At the end of this cycle, the heroine is graced with the internal and external powers that she has gained to become a medium of change and justice in the world. She becomes like the creative sorcer-ess, attributed to Tarot trump the Magician (I), where all things are possible, but only in the limited time allotted through her successful completion of the ascension process. At the successful conclusion of this cycle, the heroine has not only achieved her own internal transformation, but she has also become an integral part of her social world. She is at home, loved, and appreciated, unlike the hero in many of their mythic and literary depictions, who can never return to what was once their place in the world.

CHAPTER FOUR

INVOCATION OF PERSONAL TRANSFORMATION USING THE TAROT TRUMPS

"Whether joyous or tragic, man and cosmos hold a
dialogue in which the One grows in the one,
and one evolves in the One."
JOSEPH CAMPBELL, *Tarot Revelations* p. 284

We have fully covered the Hero's and Heroine's Journey and the cosmogonic cycle as it relates to the trumps of the Tarot, and I have named these two conjoined cycles the cycle of transformative initiation. It is, I believe, the ultimate, ongoing, and never-ending process that envelops those who have achieved the initial transformative initiation trigger.

While most of this book has focused on the scripted traditional and untraditional initiations, there is another kind of initiatory magic that is just as powerful and certainly more meaningful. Scripted initiation rites impact the outer world and the inner world, but they may only briefly touch that intrinsic and profound process of change and continual growth that is our spiritual and magical process. Our inner world, consisting of symbols, archetypes, and dynamic interactions between our self, our mind, and the outer world that make up our conscious being are ever performing a dramatic play inside our heads.

This process affects our dreams, influences our choices, and energizes our expectations throughout our lives. We cannot escape this ongoing psychic play, nor is it easy to identify and understand it without outside analysis and help. We can learn to still our thoughts and observe them, but through the artifice of the Tarot, we can identify the quality and nature of that dynamic process operating within us, and through the Tarot, learn to guide and stimulate them.

While undergoing initiation rituals and experiencing their impact, it is the Tarot that helps us see into ourselves and determine our own progress, embarked as we are on the pathways of life leading ultimately to death. The cycle of transformative initiation follows a cyclic pattern, and the first thing that we can do is to determine where we are within that pattern. The ending of a cycle can be peaceful and even blissful, but it is just the hiatus before a new cycle begins. The period between cycles may be long or short, depending on what is happening in our lives. Yet, at times, we can also potentially find ourselves stuck at a particular point in the cycle without the ability to move forward. This event, in fact, occurs more often than we might admit.

We should briefly examine the nature of this cycle and try to pinpoint the event we experienced that was traumatic enough to start it operating in the first place. It is possible that people who completely lack any self-awareness might not ever trigger their internal transformative process. For such individuals, life has a kind of monochromic quality that is only changed or shaped by external social interventions or occurrences. These individuals can never be seekers because they don't understand that there is anything to seek outside or within themselves. They are content with who they are and their role in life. Seekers have an inner hunger for knowledge, stimulus, insights, visions, and ultimately, understanding. They are not content with what life has to offer, so they restlessly travel the world and voyage within their minds to find that thing that they seem to lack.

Transformative initiation occurs only to seekers, and never to those who are content with their lot. Seekers can be either born with their rapacious curiosity, or they can be made that way by circumstance. A contented person can have their entire world or part of it destroyed and they will become, for a time or even permanently, a seeker. They could also just find another peaceful place in which to be complacent. However, at some point, a seeker will experience a powerful and profound experience that will traumatize them and trigger the transformative process. It is typically an external event, but it can be an internal and psychic event as well. Tragedies are often the triggers that start this process, but it requires the drive of a seeker to continue it by never being satisfied with the answers that they obtain.

For myself, my triggering event was when I partook of a substantial dose of LSD-25 when I was only fifteen years old. I saw and experienced things that no young teenager should ever experience, but, in fact, if I had not been a seeker, I would never have even considered taking that drug. The profound trauma that I underwent triggered my initiatory cycle, and I began my spiritual and magical path from the moment I recovered my mind after tripping for over twelve hours. It is my belief that anyone who is a seeker and has a certain degree of self-awareness will know the moment their initiatory cycle was triggered since it will be an event unlike any other and remembered for the extent of their lifetime.

I must assume that if you bought this book and you are a practicing Witch or Pagan, then you are definitively a seeker, and it is likely that you have had magical and spiritual experiences that were profoundly life-changing. You have already begun your journey and are engaged at some point in your internal psychic cycle. What you may not know is exactly at what stage you are in this endless process. The key to determining this question and opening the mystery that you truly are is through the artifice of Tarot card readings.

While astrology can explain to you the timing of the factors of the potential that can occur in your life, and even help to understand who you are, it is the Tarot that can help you determine your spiritual and magical progress on the great spiraling cyclic pathway of trans-formative initiation. Scripted initiation rites engage the mind and challenge your capabilities, so determining your spiritual and magical process and helping guide it is one of the great factors in working this kind of transformative magic. For this kind of operation, we must rely on the Tarot, and most particularly, the twenty-two cards of the Major Arcana.

Knowing the Stage
of Your Initiatory Process

The very first step in this kind of magic is founded on self-knowledge, and the key is the Tarot, as we have already discussed. Determining your stage in the initiatory process is done by doing some passive readings with the full deck of Tarot, thoroughly shuffled and randomized. The key to the puzzle is to ask the question about where you are in your initiatory process. If you never ask the question, then the answer will never be voluntarily given unless you stumble upon it while divining on another issue.

This is a serious and strategic reading that you are about to perform, so doing it in the sacred and charged space of a consecrated magic circle would be the first requirement. I would also advise that you engage in a period of meditation before doing the reading so that your mind is poised and accessible. You will also need a pen and paper or notebook, and perhaps a reference book for the Tarot cards would be a good idea. Tarot readings can sometimes be very abstruse and not easily translated, so having a book can be helpful.

Start out by writing down and then asking the question out loud. If you want to start the reading by invoking the spiritual intelligence of the Tarot whose name is Hru, asking that great angel to attend and help you with this reading, then that would be optimal. You would ask this question after summoning Hru:

"Where am I in the initiatory process?"

Perform the reading and then analyze the response. It will be highly likely that you will need to ask additional questions to clarify the first response. You will need to pay particular attention to any trump cards that appear in your reading. Those trump cards that appear should now be seen as parts or components of your cycle of transformative initiation, and they will likely give you clues about what stage in the process you currently reside.

If you aren't clear about your current overall state, then you would probably want to do a full reading on yourself before you do the reading, asking the question about your process. I typically do a Tree of Life layout to begin such an inquiry. Do the reading and then write down the positions of the cards. Once completed, you will need to fully reshuffle the deck to ready it for the big question. If you do this kind of preliminary reading on yourself, you will also want to examine it thoroughly before you ask the question about your process.

This task will take some work to complete. You will likely have to ask multiple questions after getting the first one answered. You should write down the question and then note the Tarot cards that are drawn. How I usually do this is to draw seven cards or more. If those first seven cards do not have a trump card, then continue drawing cards until a trump card appears. You should have at least seven cards in your reading—or more if it ends with a trump card. Since the reading is in a linear layout, you would read them in a linear sequence. You should carefully analyze the response and try to determine your position in the seventeen stages of the Hero or Heroine's Journey.[33] The five-stage vision or cosmogonic cycle will never be one of the identifiable cycle stages that you would occupy, and if any of those trumps appear in your reading, it will indicate that your process is being impacted by one of the mythic stages of that greater cycle.

If you don't get a clear response to your reading, there's no need to worry because there is a magical ritual that you can work on that will help reveal the stage in the cycle that you currently occupy. The purpose of this first step was to teach you that the Tarot can be used to illuminate internalized psychic processes that are going on but might not be in your conscious awareness yet. Doing this reading will trigger an internal process, so even if the answer from the card reading is unclear, you can perform a pathworking ritual that allows you to travel into the underworld itself and more directly get the answer that you are seeking.

---

33   Distinguishing between the Hero's or Heroine's Journey will have to do with the severity of your present experience with life and your possibility of forward progress. Intensity is a guide, as is whether you feel isolated or surrounded by potential helpers.

The ritual that I am going to introduce to you is called the Double Tetrahedral Gateway Vortex, and it is used to actualize both passive Tarot inquiries as well as activate ones that could trigger an internal psychic response, pushing you into the next stage of your initiatory process. This is an important ritual since it facilitates performing ritualized pathworking with one or more of the twenty-two trumps of the Major Arcana.

Ritual Tarot Pathworking

Performing the ritual Tarot pathworking using the Double Tetrahedral Gateway Vortex ritual does not require selecting a date or time based on the planetary days or hours. This is a ritual working that is performed without a lot of preparation or forethought. The decision to perform this work is based on necessity and an intuitive need to know and understand your own internal process at that moment. Knowing who you are is one important objective, but knowing where you are going is the other. Together, they help you understand yourself and your life's path, and anyone who has this knowledge is far ahead of those who are without this kind of strategic insight.

As far as the phase of the moon is concerned, I typically like doing these workings when the moon is waning or new, since at those times of the night, the psychic atmosphere is quiet and relatively peaceful, which is quite unlike the psychic atmosphere when the moon is gibbous or full. However, you can perform this rite whenever you need to understand something about your own process, so the best time to do this working is when you feel the need to do it.

Before you start, I would recommend that you observe the basic ritual preparations, such as taking a bath, donning your robes, anointing yourself, consecrating a magic circle, and then engaging in a period of meditation. Make certain that you have isolated the trumps in your Tarot deck and that you have selected one or more of them for your pathworking. You should have your notebook, pen, and a book on the Tarot cards to consult during the working. You might write down your preliminary questions and objectives, and the trump card that you wish to inquire about.

The ritual is called the Double Tetrahedral Gateway because the typical three-point gateway that we have used in previous rituals will get a fourth point in the zenith, and when all the lines of the triangle are connected to the zenith, it will form a tetrahedral structure. There will be such a gateway for the west to enter the underworld domain, and one to the east to exit the underworld domain and enter the waking world. The double tetrahedral gates are surrounded by a rose-ankh vortex structure, which we have also seen in the other rituals. The operator draws an inner circle within the underworld domain, and that is the place where the Tarot inquiry and pathworking are to be performed.

To decorate the gateway points, you can use three selected trump cards placed at each of them so that the three gateway points are qualified by the three cards. If you take this approach, then the selection of the trump-qualified gate keys would represent the guide, guardian, and ordeal of your initiatory process. You can pick them out if you happen to know them, or you can be very brave and randomly select them, letting chance and fate guide the selection. I have often used this approach because it does seem to help me define my initiatory process.

You will do the same operation to determine the guide, guardian, and ordeal for the return, and these cards will adorn the gateway points for the eastern gate. You will have to set up the western gate with the selected or randomly drawn cards before the ritual is performed, but you will have to switch the gate keys to the eastern orientation with their associated cards before beginning to erect the eastern gateway tetrahedral structure and passing through the return portal.

The Tarot trump that is to be the focus of the pathworking is either pre-selected based on prior divination or it can be randomly selected during the working. You can present either one card in this working or three cards. If you draw three cards, then they will sequentially represent the prior initiatory stage, the current stage, and the stage yet to be entered. The idea is that you will want to fully understand what these cards are imparting to you, but also, by focusing on them, you are activating their magical qualities and their associated part in your initiatory process.

Double Tetrahedral
Gateway Vortex Ritual

Now that we have discussed the function and the parts of the ritual, let us examine the actual ritual pattern so that you can fully grasp how this ritual would proceed.

1. Using the wand, proceed to the northern watchtower, and therein draw a rose-ankh before it, projecting into it a deep violet color.
2. Proceed to the western watchtower and do the same.
3. Proceed to the southern watchtower and do the same.
4. Proceed to the eastern watchtower and do the same.
5. Proceed to the center of the circle and draw a rose-ankh to the nadir, projecting into it a deep violet color.
6. Return the wand to the altar, take the sword, and proceed to the northern watchtower. Using the sword, draw a line of force from the ankh in the watchtower to the ankh in the center of the circle at the nadir.
7. Proceed to the western watchtower, use the sword, and do the same.
8. Proceed to the southern watchtower, use the sword, and do the same.
9. Proceed to the eastern watchtower, use the sword, and do the same.
10. Return the sword to the altar and pick up the wand. Proceed to the northern watchtower and starting from there, proceed to walk around the circle widdershins, and slowly arc into the center of the circle, passing the northern watchtower three times, and holding the wand out to push the forces to the center of the circle. Once reaching the center, push the combined powers into the nadir. The invoking vortex is now set.
11. Return the wand to the altar. Proceed to the eastern watchtower and face the west.
12. Draw invoking spirals to the southeast, northeast, and then the western watchtower to the Tarot trumps placed there—these positions are the guide, guardian, and ordeal

respectively—address each and their Tarot-based process when drawing the invoking spiral.

13. Draw a lesser hexagram of union (earth) in the zenith and visualize it shining rays of light down to the circle floor, illuminating it.

14. Draw lines of force with the right hand, from the northeast angle to the western watchtower, to the southeast angle, and then back again to the northeast angle. Then draw each gateway point to the hexagram in the zenith, forming a tetrahedral. The tetrahedral gateway is established.

15. Proceed to walk slowly from the east to the west, and when arriving at the west, perform the pantomime of opening the veil or a curtain with a dramatic flourish. Step close into the western watchtower and turn to face the east, performing the descending wave of energy from above the head to the feet.

16. Proceed to walk slowly from west to east, imagining descending into a chamber—stop at the center of the circle where there is placed the central altar.

17. Draw an inner circle, starting in the north and proceeding widdershins around the circle until ending again at the north. Retrieve a notebook, pen, and the selected Tarot card or cards from the altar and proceed to the center circle, stepping into it.

18. Sit in the central circle and then lay out the card or cards on the floor—begin the internal inquiry by silently summoning the Angel Hru, who presides over the Tarot.

19. Sit in deep meditation, asking the written question (if more than one, then one at a time) and focusing all your attention on the Tarot cards. When any kind of response is sensed or any insight is perceived, write it down in the notebook. If there are three cards to be used, then they will represent the state prior to the present, the present, and the future.

20. Once there is clarity on the Tarot inquiry and all questions have been answered, say the following:

"I use my will to make this clear directive a part of my initiatory process! So Mote it Be!"

21. When the meditative communion with the Angel of the Tarot is completed, then stand before up in the central circle, bow, and give the presiding Tarot intelligence a warm farewell and thanks for visiting.

22. Proceed to the west, stand before the watchtower, and perform the pantomime gesture of closing a veil or curtain. Then draw sealing spirals over each of the gateway points.

23. Take the three Tarot cards from their positions for the western gateway and set them up for the eastern gateway. (NW, E, SW)

24. Then proceed to the west, then turn again to face the east.

25. Draw invoking spirals to the northwest, southwest, and then the eastern watchtower to the gate keys and their selected Tarot trumps—these positions are the guide, guardian, and ordeal respectively—spiral.[34]

26. Draw a lesser hexagram of union (earth) in the zenith, visualize it shining rays of light down to the circle floor, illuminating it.

27. Draw lines of force with the right hand, from the northwest angle to the eastern watchtower, to the southwest angle, and then back again to the northwest angle. Then draw each gateway point to the hexagram in the zenith, forming a tetrahedral. The tetrahedral gateway is established.

28. Proceed to walk slowly from the west to the east, and when arriving at the east, perform the pantomime of opening the veil or a curtain with a dramatic flourish. Step close into the eastern watchtower and turn to face the west, performing the descending wave of energy from above the head to the feet.

29. Proceed to walk slowly from east to west, imagining ascending out of a chamber—stop at the center of the circle.

30. Take up the wand, proceed to the eastern watchtower, and draw therein a sealing spiral.

31. Proceed to the southern watchtower and draw a sealing spiral.

32. Proceed to the western watchtower and draw a sealing spiral.

---

34 These would be the same personages that oversaw the western gateway.

33. Proceed to the northern watchtower and draw a sealing spiral.
34. Return the wand to the altar. The ritual is completed.

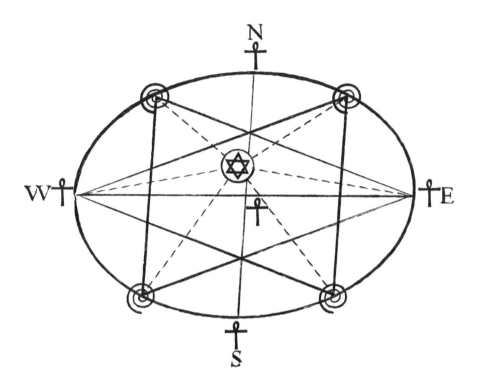

Diagram of the Double Tetrahedral Gate Vortex Rite.

The above ritual pattern might be simplistic, but it is very effective at helping to determine and trigger an initiatory process. It has both a passive and active use for Tarot trumps, and I have found that it produces effects that are quite profound and astonishing for such a simple and brief rite. Of course, the power of this ritual is to be found in the cards of the Major Arcana itself since they represent the stages that we undergo throughout our lives and are imbued with the symbols of transformation. They are particularly potent once the initiatory process is started.

INITIATION AND TRANSFORMATION IN MODERN WITCHCRAFT

"There are a number of fragmentary accounts of old-time Witch initiations, and from these a composite picture can be built up. The whole-hearted acceptance of the Witch religion, and the oath of loyalty, were the main features."
DOREEN VALIENTE

We have traversed the full spectrum of phenomena and the utility of Witchcraft initiations. We have learned that there are scripted initiations that are adopted, whether by tradition or by invention, and we have also learned about the phenomenon of transformative initiations, or processes that produce profound changes in individuals. I believe that I have shown that transformations and initiations are not always simultaneous occurrences and that a powerful transformation can happen to someone even if they have never received a traditional initiation.

What this distinction has produced over a period of several decades is an inequality between strict traditional Witches and their adherents, and an ever-increasing population of self-initiated Witches who have, for various reasons, decided not to undergo a traditional initiation. As time progresses, the number of self-initiated non-traditional Witches will continue to grow, and perhaps the old traditions will be diminished until they no longer exist. People want to access and engage with Witchcraft as both a religion and a system of magic without having to endure the politics and prejudices of traditional practicing covens. That is always a risk when joining a traditional coven.

Securing favor and proving one's worthiness can be quite a bottleneck to being able to be initiated into a coven. I believe that this is one of several reasons why there are more self-initiated Witches than those who can boast of an impressive pedigree. The pioneer women and men who were first initiated into Witchcraft in the 1960s and 70s are dying off, leaving behind a hollowed-out organization. What the future holds for traditional Witchcraft is anyone's guess. Coven-based traditions could make a comeback, but such organizations would have to admit the self-taught and the self-initiated into their groups. I have doubts that such a thing would be allowed, at least by today's adherents of traditional Witchcraft orthodoxy.

Ultimately, an initiation of the transformative type would be the only arbiter of the worthiness or authenticity of a practicing Witch. That kind of process, as we have seen, would be more likely to occur if the practitioner had a profound encounter with one of the Witchcraft Deities, whether by design or by accident. It is the Deities whose powers and wisdom decree who is an authentic practitioner or one who is a pretender, and this is true, whether the practitioner is a traditional Witch or self-initiated. As elders and long-time residents of the path of transformative initiation, we can know another soul who is walking on the path with us and engage with them if that is the collective will of the moment. However, it is becoming more difficult to measure the worthiness of a Witch, except by the quality and depth of their worship and magical workings.

Our traditions and practices are changing. Already, things are not like they were when I was just starting out five decades ago. That is not very long for the life of a religion, even one as new as Modern Witchcraft. I have seen the practice of Witchcraft start out as an obscure religious and magical tradition back in the 1970s, when many people knew each other, like living in a small village. I could go to Pagan festivals and meet the people who started it all back in the 60s. Many of those people are now dead and departed (but not forgotten). Now, in the present age, Witchcraft is one of the fastest-growing religions in the nation, which is ironic considering the pressures that the Evangelical Christian movement and the religious right have put into trying to stomp out this new religion.

Wherever we go from this time forward should include the rituals and practices that I have outlined in my five books. A Witchcraft religion without a solid magical practice would be a religion that is empty, dry, and exceptionally boring. Magic is the juice that keeps Witchcraft a fascinating practice, keeping it relevant to our post-modern age. While traditional initiations and practices will likely continue to be used in some manner for the foreseeable future, I believe that transformative initiation is the likely candidate for the future of Modern Witchcraft.

Perhaps the most relevant topic that I have written about in this book is the one where I can link the Hero's Journey with the initiation cycle, including the Heroine's Journey, to the twenty-two trumps of the Major Arcana of the Tarot. Using the Tarot trumps to visualize the cycle of transformative initiation is probably one of the most important tools that I have offered to the practitioner of Witchcraft magic. These Tarot cards have become the veritable symbols of transformation that activate both scripted and unscripted initiations. A Witch can use the Tarot to determine their place in that cycle or trigger a stalled process and help resolve internal issues before they erupt into painful complexes and borderline psychotic episodes.

In this book, I have offered to the practitioner something that few other books have offered, which is the means to ensure that a self-initiation has depth and power that is in line with what traditional initiations as practiced by covens might be able to provide. It delivers the tools to trigger and instigate a transformative initiation, and to determine the stage where one currently resides in that cycle.

The past two years (2022–2023) were very interesting for me, particularly concerning my writing endeavors with Witchcraft and ritual magic. I had completed my book *Talismanic Magic for Witches* and started to go through the process of revising it, submitting the final revised manuscript to Llewellyn for production. I also wrote and completed *Sacramental Theurgy for Witches* and I submitted that project to Crossed Crow Books at the end of March 2023, where it will go through its revision process and ultimately into production.

I have also completed writing the final book in that series, which has the title *Transformative Initiation for Witches*, and I should be able to submit that manuscript before the end of autumn 2023. There will be, once the last two books go through production and end up in print, five books in the *For Witches* series. The cover colors are related to gemstone-type hues, with the series represented in published sequences by onyx, amber, amethyst, emerald, and garnet. I am looking forward to walking into a lecture event or a book signing someday with all five books tucked under my arm. It is quite an achievement and one that started in 2016.

Why did I write this series of books? I have put seven years of my life into researching, developing, and writing them, and they are all books with the traditional Witch or Pagan audience in mind. You might ask me the question, *"Aren't there enough books out in the public for the Witchcraft or Pagan community? Why do we need more of this kind of literature when the publishing world appears to be saturated with this media topic?"*

To answer this question, you must look at what is out there in the public domain. There are a lot of good books, but none of them cover the kind of advanced magical workings that my series touches on. The areas that I wanted to address in my books have to do with the magical and religious initiative of the individual Witch or Pagan seeking to perform more advanced kinds of magical workings that are just as cutting-edge and relevant as what the ceremonial magical community is currently performing.

These works of mine will allow the Witch or Pagan to either access the work currently occurring in the magical community, such as with newly translated grimoires or historical research in the areas of magic and Witchcraft, or to build their own independent and comparable magical systems.

It was my objective and hope that the reader of my books would work to build up their own magical system extended off the baseline traditions of modern Witchcraft and Pagan magic. It is the path that I forged back in the late 1970s and early 1980s, and it is very relevant today because I continued to develop these methodologies over the years. I have not been resting on my imaginary laurels. I have continued to reinvent my magic over the decades so that what I am presenting today is as fresh as it was forty years ago.

So, that is the answer to why I worked to write these five books. A deeper reason is that I had the pride and arrogance to believe that what I had started to develop years ago was an important contribution to the practice of Witchcraft magic, despite the absolute plethora of books in print now and for the foreseeable future. It is my legacy to pull together this lore and present it in an organized and accessible media for all interested parties to examine, and hopefully, to adopt some of it in their own workings. It is my belief and hope that such a prideful journey is not hopelessly corrupted by my own hubris, as is the case with many human endeavors to capture a lifetime of work in a mere series of books.

To answer the question of what I wrote, I can elucidate that answer here. There were, in my estimation, five different areas that were missing from the canon of magical lore in the modern Witchcraft traditions. None of these methodologies are to be found in the traditional Book of Shadows. The five areas are as follows:

1. (ONYX) SPIRIT CONJURATION: Including the acquiring of a familiar spirit and the mastery of the domain of spirit, ancestor worship, building a shrine of spirits and demigods, communicating with the spirits, accessing the spirit world, appropriating, and making use of the old grimoires in one's magic.

2. (AMBER) ADVANCED ENERGY MAGIC: Working with the four elements as the sixteen Elemental Spirits and forty Qualified Powers, developing energy structures beyond the cone of power to include the Pyramid of Power, magical Octagon, sigil creation, and other energy model of magic constructs.

3. (AMETHYST) TALISMANIC MAGIC: Working planetary and zodiacal magic, using the septagram to invoke and establish planetary intelligences, developing the mechanism to generate talismans, using the lunar mansions, zodiacal decans and septans, and performing celestial magic within a strict observance of the planetary day, hour, and associated astrological auspices.

4. (EMERALD) SACRAMENTAL THEURGY: Enhancing the religious elements of Witchcraft magic to bring them into the ritual workings, godhead assumption reformation and full godhead personification, consecration rites of the mass, the benediction, and the Great Rite, creating sacred magical artifacts, animating statues or paintings with the essence of a godhead, operating within a sacred and magical grove, and the assembling and performance of the Grand Sabbat.

5. (GARNET) TRANSFORMATIVE INITIATION: Differences between the scripted initiation rites and the process of psychological transformation, initiations beyond and below

the traditional three, madness and enlightenment, the dark night of the soul and its mitigation, the twenty-two stages of the Hero's Journey as the cycle of transformative initiation, the stages of the Heroine's Journey, harnessing the cycle of initiation to enhance and empower constructive forms of internal and external transformation, and the key to spiritual evolution in the Witchcraft tradition.

These are the five areas that I address in the five books that are a part of the *For Witches* series. I believe that any Witch from any of the various traditions should be able to make use of the lore in these books, and thereby enhance and expand their magical and liturgical work to include areas that are not typically defined in these traditions. The test will be relevant within the tradition that one is following, the desire for more advanced methodologies and techniques of magic, and the need to have a greater magical and liturgical impact within one's mind, coven or group, or community at large. These books are not for everyone, and of course, some or all of them might not be relevant. However, for the typical magical practitioner who is also a Witch or Pagan, I believe that these books will help to build a more complete tradition, filling in the gaps that may exist in these practices.

I believe that this book, the last in this series, is one of the most important since it is the last of the areas not covered by either traditional Witchcraft practices or the advanced lore that I have learned and mastered over the years. I expect to see all five books together in print by the end of 2024, and I will have completed all the tasks that I set out to do, or at least as I envisioned them back in 2016.

While I did not anticipate five books in total, I knew that this series would fill in the gaps that I had to develop nearly fifty years ago. I am glad that my muse drew me through this intricate maze to help me produce these five books, and I look forward to when I can start writing other books in another series, to build on the legacy that I have established in my literary journey that started over thirty years ago.

May these five books and the blessings of the Goddesses and Gods of Witchcraft and Paganism be always with you.

Frater Barrabbas

BIBLIOGRAPHY

Apuleius, *The Golden Ass*. Translated by E. J. Kenney. Penguin Classics, 1999 (originally second century).

Baum, L. Frank. *The Wizard of Oz*. Geroge M. Hill Company, 1900.

Campbell, Joseph. *The Hero with a Thousand Faces*. New World Library, 2008.

Carriger, Gail. *The Heroine's Journey—For Writers, Readers, and Fans of Pop Culture*. Gail Carriger LLC, 2020 (Self Published).

Crowley, Aleister, et al. *Thoth Tarot Deck, Ordo Templi Orientis*. U.S. Game Systems, Inc., 1969.

de la Cruz, San Juan. *The Dark Night Of The Soul; La Noche Oscura del Alma*. Creative Media Partners, LLC, 2018 (originally sixteenth-century).

Duncan, Malcomb C. *Duncan's Ritual of Freemasonry*. Crown Publishers, 1866.

Editorial Staff, "Initiation," *Merriam Online Dictionary*, https://www.merriam-webster.com/dictionary/initiation. Accessed February 12, 2023

Fitzgerald, F. Scott. *The Crack-Up*. New Directions, 1945.

Fortune, Dion. *The Esoteric Orders and Their Work*. United Kingdom: Occult Book Society, 1928.

Frater Barrabbas. *Sacramental Theurgy for Witches*. Crossed Crow Books, 2023.

——. *Talismanic Magic for Witches*. Llewellyn Publications, 2023.

——. *Elemental Powers for Witches*. Llewellyn Publications, 2021.

——. *Spirit Conjuring for Witches*. Llewellyn Publications, 2017.

——. *Mastering the Art of Ritual Magic—Omnibus Edition*. Megalithica Books—Immanion Press, 2013.

Gia Fu, Feng. *Tao Te Ching: Text Only Edition*. Vintage Books—Random House, Inc, 2012.

"Information about Mental Illness and the Brain—NIH Curriculum Supplement Series—NCBI Bookshelf." *National Center for Biotechnology Information*, https://www.ncbi.nlm.nih.gov/books/NBK20369/. Accessed 11 Oct. 2023.

Jeffers, H. Paul. *Freemasons—Inside the World's Oldest Secret Society*. Citadel Press, 2005.

Johnson, Robert A. *She—Understanding Feminine Psychology*. Harper Perennial, 2020.

Kelly, Aidan A. *Inventing Witchcraft—A Case Study in the Creation of a New Religion*. Thoth Publications, 2007.

McKeown, Trevor W. "Gerald Brosseau Gardner." *Grand Lodge of British Columbia and Yukon*, Grand Lodge of British Columbia and Yukon, https://freemasonry.bcy.ca/biography/esoterica/gardner_g/gardner_g.html.

"Mental Disorders." *World Health Organization (WHO)*, https://www.who.int/news-room/fact-sheets/detail/mental-disorders. Accessed 12 Oct. 2023.

"Mental Health Video Resource Library, NAMI: National Alliance on Mental Illness." *NAMI: National Alliance on Mental Illness*, https://www.nami.org/Support-Education/Video-Resource-Library/What-is-Depression.

"Psychedelic Medicine: A Re-Emerging Therapeutic Paradigm—PMC." *PubMed Central (PMC)*, https://www.ncbi.nlm.nih.gov/pmc/articles/PMC4592297/. Accessed 12 Oct. 2023.

Smith, Pamela C. and Arthur Edward Waite. *Rider Waite Tarot Deck*. U.S. Games Systems, Inc, 1910.

Tatar, Maria. *The Heroine with 1,001 Faces*. Liveright Publishing Corporation, 2021.

"The World Health Report 2001: Mental Disorders Affect One in Four People." *World Health Organization (WHO)*, https://www.who.int/news/item/28-09-2001-the-world-health-report-2001-mental-disorders-affect-one-in-four-people. Accessed 12 Oct. 2023.

Willard, Nancy. *East of the Sun and West of the Moon*. Harcourt, Brace, Jovanovich, 1989.

INDEX

A

Air, 42, 47, 55, 91–92, 94–95, 99–100
Alexandrian, 14, 29, 41, 43–44
Archetypal, 18, 66, 94, 106–107, 114, 122, 124, 126–127, 132, 135, 139, 145–146, 149, 151, 155–157

B

Blindfold, 20, 23–24, 29, 35, 37, 40
Book of Shadows, 26, 29, 31, 35, 41, 177
Boon, 125, 127–128, 136–138, 142–143, 145, 151
British Traditional Witchcraft, 1, 13, 17

C

Compromise, 150–151, 158–159
Cosmogonic Cycle, 4, 9, 55, 91, 93, 121–123, 125–127, 129, 136–141, 145, 151, 153–154, 161, 165

Coven, 1–3, 5, 13–15, 17–18, 23–24, 29, 31, 33, 38, 43–45, 52, 62, 69–78, 80, 82–83, 86, 89–90, 92, 106, 109, 146, 173, 175, 178
Croning, 86

D

Dark Night of the Soul, 108, 111–116, 118, 178
Death, 4, 7–8, 15, 25, 27, 29, 32, 37–38, 40–41, 47–48, 51, 55, 66–67, 77, 87, 91, 93, 98–99, 106–111, 122–125, 128, 131–132, 139–141, 153, 155–158, 162
Dedicant, 78–80
Dedication, 2, 48, 56, 72–73, 76–79, 89–90, 92–93
Depression, 108, 112, 116–118

E

Earth, 38, 42, 47, 55, 62–65, 84, 91–92, 94–96, 98, 100, 121–122, 138–139, 154, 169–170

Elixir, 127–128, 136
Entered Apprentice, 18, 20–21, 25–26, 76
Eros, 126, 150, 153, 156, 158

F

Fellow craft, 18, 20–21, 23, 25–27, 41
Fifth degree, 42–43, 51–53, 58–59, 90–91
Fire, 42, 47, 55, 91–92, 94–96, 98, 100, 138, 144
First degree, 15, 17, 21, 32, 42, 78, 92
Fisher King, 142–143
Fool's Journey, 123–126
Four elements, 42, 82–83, 89–91, 93–95, 102, 138, 177
Fourth degree, 42–45, 50, 52, 93

G

Gardner, 5, 18–20, 25–26, 29, 44
Gardnerian, 1, 14, 18, 29, 43, 62, 69, 77–78
Gate, 38, 40, 46, 54, 97, 167, 170–171
Great Rite, 17, 26, 28, 30–31, 33, 36, 42, 45, 65, 177
Grove, 38, 40, 79, 92–93, 177
Guardian, 34, 37–39, 43, 46, 49, 51, 54, 56–57, 59–60, 97, 101, 127, 131, 142, 167–168, 170

H

Healing, 63, 92, 124, 139, 142–143, 150, 155
Hero with a Thousand Faces, 121, 123, 126–127, 136

Hero's Journey, 5, 9, 121–133, 135–137, 141, 143, 145, 149–151, 153, 175, 178
Heroine's Journey, 121, 126, 149–151, 153–154, 161, 165, 175, 178
Hierophant, 43, 51, 56, 63–64, 66–67, 144, 159
Hiram Abiff, 26–28

I

Initiatory process, 31, 42, 82, 116, 146, 164, 166–167, 169, 171
Internal psychic change, 8, 73, 106

L

Love, 25, 29, 32, 36, 38–40, 47, 77, 79, 84, 97, 106, 133, 153, 156–157

M

Major Arcana, 123, 145, 163, 166, 171, 175
Mason, 20, 24, 26–29
Masonic, 18–21, 23, 25–26, 76
Master, 1, 5, 8–9, 14–15, 17, 20–21, 23–24, 26–29, 41–44, 52, 57, 61, 66–67, 83, 93, 119, 132, 137, 144, 146
Mental illness, 108–111, 118
Mentor, 85, 150, 155
Monarch, 51, 56, 62–63, 65, 155
Mystery, 3, 5–6, 10, 14–15, 17, 19, 21, 23, 25–29, 32–33, 35, 37, 39–40, 42–43, 45–67,

89–90, 92, 97–98, 100–101, 106, 121–122, 124, 128, 135, 138, 144, 154, 163

O

Oath, 2, 9, 17, 21, 24, 28, 34, 76–77, 79, 173
Ordeal, 1–2, 4, 13–15, 17–20, 23–26, 28–33, 37, 41–45, 47, 49–50, 52, 54, 57, 81, 91, 93, 95–99, 101–102, 107, 109, 114, 117, 123, 127, 131–133, 135, 140, 142, 157–158, 167–168, 170

P

Pathworking, 165–167
Priest, 1, 17, 29, 31, 33, 35–37, 43, 51–52, 56, 59, 61, 65, 70, 92
Priestess, 1, 5, 14, 17, 29, 31, 33, 37, 43, 51–52, 56, 59, 62, 70, 130–131, 141, 156
Process, 2–9, 15, 25, 27–28, 31, 42, 44, 51, 72, 74–75, 78, 80–83, 85, 90–91, 94, 105–117, 119, 121, 123–124, 129, 133–134, 136–137, 139, 142, 144, 146, 149, 155, 157–167, 169, 171, 173–175, 177
Psyche, 7–8, 51, 81–82, 107–108, 123, 126, 150, 153, 156, 158
Pyramid, 31, 45–46, 53–54, 95, 97, 177

R

Rebirth, 4, 8, 15, 25, 27, 29, 32, 34, 37–38, 40, 51, 107–111, 121–123, 140–141

S

Scourging, 20, 25
Scripted initiation, 5–10, 69, 80–83, 109, 121, 161, 163, 173, 177
Second degree, 14–15, 21, 23, 25, 30, 32, 42, 92
Self-initiation, 8, 72, 80, 82–83, 89–91, 94–95, 175
Senex, 86
St. John of the Cross, 114
Symbols of transformation, 5–6, 8–9, 17–19, 107, 121, 125, 145, 171, 175

T

Tao, 51, 136–137
Third degree, 5, 14–15, 26–29, 31–32, 36, 41–42, 45, 92
Transformative Initiation, 4–5, 7–9, 80, 90, 105, 110, 116, 118, 121, 123–124, 146, 161–164, 173–175, 177–178
Trust, 32, 40, 106, 110

W

Water, 42, 45, 48, 55, 60, 91, 93–96, 99–100, 138–140, 142, 144
Witch Queen, 3, 37, 43, 62